T0285758

Frances PERKINS
CHAMPION OF AMERICAN WORKERS

Ruth Cashin Monsell

Frances
PERKINS
CHAMPION OF AMERICAN WORKERS

HISTRIA
YA

HistriaYA

Las Vegas ◊ Chicago ◊ Palm Beach

Published in the United States of America by
Histria Books,
7181 N. Hualapai Way, Ste. 130-86
Las Vegas, NV 89166 USA
HistriaBooks.com

HistriaYA is an imprint of Histria Books dedicated to incredible books for Young Adult readers. Titles published under the various imprints of Histria Books are distributed worldwide.

Library of Congress Control Number: 2023948280

ISBN 978-1-59211-387-3 (hardcover)
ISBN 978-1-59211-409-2 (eBook)

Contents

This book is dedicated with love to Frances Perkins' only grandchild, Tomlin Perkins Coggeshall, the first person to inspire its writing, with thanks for his friendship and his unfailing enthusiasm, encouragement, stories, insights, and practical support.

I also dedicate it to my outstanding sons and grandsons, and to the memory of my mother, who encouraged me to write and illustrate my first chapter book, the biography of our Siamese cat, at age ten.

Foreword

In the summer of 2012, I read in my local newspaper about an upcoming tour nearby. It would take me into the home of an *extremely* important woman in American history. She was the true architect and driving force, I read, behind the New Deal. I was thunderstruck by this idea! Like most people, I always credited President Franklin Delano Roosevelt with the programs that led America out of the Great Depression. I believed we had Social Security, Unemployment Insurance, the minimum wage, and all the rest of "the social safety net," because of FDR and those he led to implement it.

But on the tour, led by Frances Perkins' only grandchild, I learned the facts. Those critically important innovations were the brainchild of a woman I'd never even heard about. I was sure she hadn't been in those short paragraphs about women — you know, Clara Barton, Susan B. Anthony, Harriet Tubman, Jane Addams — in my school history books. But here was this person who changed our society and gave us so much, LEFT OUT! It made me curious. And outraged.

In my questioning of well-educated adults, I repeatedly found that though we all benefit from her contributions, almost no one knew what those were. They didn't even know her name.

The spark was lit that day that led to this book. I desperately wanted to bring her nearly hidden story out into the limelight. After reading the few biographies I could find on her, some no longer in print, I began to write.

So: WELCOME to the story of a true American Superhero — and a nearly forgotten one!

Introducing Frances

Her name was Frances Perkins, and her crusade to improve the lives of all Americans began before women even had the right to vote. This is her inspiring story. May it inspire *you!*

She was born into a conservative, solidly middle-class family in 1880, the daughter of a merchant who owned a printing and stationery store.

There was no inherited family wealth.

She was not an outstanding student.

She never had a benefactor or a formal mentor.

She was not gifted from the start with great beauty, charm, wit, or confidence.

Her husband was not able to work, making her the sole breadwinner for her family.

How did she do it? Where did her drive to right great wrongs come from? How did she overcome all the obstacles in her path? What inspired her along the way? Read on!

While you read, you'll encounter these items along the way. All represent something significant in this great woman's life:

A late-night raid

A visiting speaker

A severed hand

A colonial era homestead on the river

Night stalkers

A boy arrested and jailed

A drawerful of cockroaches

A devastating fire

A stockpile of explosives

Rosie the Riveter

A man with a gun

An impeachment hearing

An invitation to live with 27 young men

A man with a knife

A tricorn hat

Chapter 1

Fire!

Burnt and broken bodies littered the sidewalk, limbs twisted in all directions. There were over fifty of the them, in one place piled so thick their falls broke the pavement. They lay awaiting transport to the morgue, a tangle of long hair, braids, rumpled cotton dresses and aprons and high button shoes. Almost all of them were girls and women in their teens and twenties.

They had leapt to their deaths from the top floor windows of a building swept by a flash fire. It was the infamous Triangle Shirtwaist Factory in New York City.

Among the first eye witnesses at the site was a young woman with her face tear-stained. But in her heart grew red-hot anger. She knew this horrific disaster could have been prevented. She knew, better than anyone else, that it was destined to occur. She had been inspecting such workplaces since she was in college, and had just completed an extensive report on fire hazards in the mills and textile factories of the city.

By the time all the remaining bodies trapped inside the building were found, the count stood at 146 lives lost. All but seventeen were young and female.

The young woman unflinchingly witnessing it all was Frances Perkins. She knew that what she had seen would be seared on her mind and heart forever. She resolved to spend her life fighting the conditions that could permit such a tragedy. Frances believed that this day could become a torch to light up the sky of industry reform everywhere in the country.

Chapter 2: Maine Magic

The journey from Worcester, Massachusetts to Newcastle, Maine was an agonizingly slow trip of over 200 miles for a girl of twelve. She watched with fidgety impatience at the window of the train for her first glimpses of the state she so loved.

"Papa, *please*...," she begged, "how much longer?"

"Oh, only about another couple of hours now, Fannie," he replied. Then he smiled softly as he watched his eldest daughter's shoulders and face droop in disappointment.

She began to spot white church steeples piercing the blue sky. Little dories and fishing boats still bobbed in the quaint harbors while seagulls soared and swooped, sometimes seeming to do cartwheels in the air. Now she was starting to see more towering pine and spruce trees. She longed to again fill her lungs with their clean, woodsy scent.

The trip had taken an eternity! All the way she daydreamed about the delights summer held in store. Arriving in Maine each summer felt magical, like her birthday and Christmas morning rolled into one, or a full-mooned starry night in June with fireflies twinkling through the trees. Anticipation rose in her chest, feeling fluttery as though a little bird were flapping in there, and she giggled. Wrapping her arms around her shoulders, she gave herself a squeeze of sheer delight.

Finally, the train pulled into the little Newcastle station, and soon the family and all their luggage were in the carriage which would carry them "home." Just a few miles more. But to young Fannie (her given name, before she changed it to Frances) the horses, plodding along in the afternoon sunshine, seemed painfully slow. Excitement, and eagerness to hug her Grandmother, Cynthia Otis Perkins, bubbled up in her. She couldn't wait to be back in the old, sprawling family homestead, a hundred-acre saltwater farm on the Damariscotta River that had been in the Perkins family for generations — in fact, since colonial days. She could already smell the tang of salt air and pine. She caught a glimpse of late day sunbeams dancing on the water in the harbor, and a few stately ships at their moorings. Each one gave her joy.

At long last, the horses pulled into the drive, and there it was: "The Brick House," her favorite place on earth, with its attached woodshed, carriage house, and big red barn, looking just as it had every summer of her life. This was the day, each year, that the two halves of her life met. It stitched together the often tedious routines and disciplines of school and home in the city, well inland, and the fun and freedom of summer on the water at her grandparents' home on the coast of Maine.

This young girl and her grandmother were soul mates. Grandma Perkins was not just a loving adult presence, but a sensible and wise one. Unlike most adults, she really listened when you talked with her. And she would reply as though to a grownup. When Grandma Perkins spoke, Fannie not only heard, but remembered. Though they saw each other rarely when it wasn't summertime, throughout her life Frances would credit her grandmother for her words of wisdom, guidance, and inspiration. She quoted her often.

Without waiting for her parents to object, Fannie jumped down from the wagon and ran to the side door, where she hoped her grandmother was waiting. And she was.

Fannie swooped in and threw her arms around grandma's middle in a big squeeze. Not very much given to impulsive shows of emotion, her grandmother was somewhat taken aback. But Mrs. Perkins recovered her breath, laughed, straightened her round wire-rimmed spectacles, held her granddaughter by the shoulders at arm's length and said just what grandmothers everywhere say: "*My, how you've grown!*"

Oh, it was going to be a *wonderful* summer: lots of time with her cousin Nan, who happened to be her best friend; days of exploring the woods (with some excellent climbing trees), or playing hide-and-seek and bandits in and around the barn and the abandoned site of the original homestead. Even work was fun on the farm, especially collecting eggs from the henhouse, which always seemed to her like a treasure hunt. There would be hours of riding a horse bareback through the fields, having lunch out on the "Picnic Rocks" surrounded by stone walls, acting out adventure stories around the two big boulders known as the Split Rock, and picking blueberries. Oh! And best of all, she'd be spending time on her river (well, she *thought* of it as hers), where, tucked into the shore, there were always a small rowboat, a sailboat, and a canoe to set off in on watery explorations.

Worcester, Massachusetts was home, and it suited her just fine. She'd never been unhappy in any of the houses they'd lived in there. It was where her school and church and friends were. But compared to the farm in Maine, with acres of freedom, it was dull. Fannie preferred grass under her feet to gravel. She loved to inhale the heady scent of the roses, lilacs, and lavender in the garden, and the aromas of treats baked in the winter kitchen beehive stove. Fannie's mouth watered as she thought of her favorite dessert: Summer Pudding, made with lots of fresh fruit and cream, served cold. It was fun to watch the big blocks of ice being delivered to the ice house, and a portion hacked off for their kitchen icebox. Summers in Worcester could be hot and gritty; in Maine on the river it always felt cooler and breezier, the air sweet and pungent, the stars stunningly bright. The neighbors, mostly other farming families, were warm and down-to-earth. She even delighted in their Maine accents, and favorite term of agreement: "Ayuh!"

Exploring the brickyard down by the river always fascinated her. It made her feel that she was stepping backward in time. Her family had proudly been making those sturdy red bricks from clay in the river bank for nearly a hundred years, and along the route into the village, she could see houses built from them. In the picture-perfect village of Damariscotta, they made up most of the bigger buildings, interspersed with white clapboard houses. She was especially proud that bricks from her own family's brickyard had been donated to build the Congregational church in Newcastle where she went to services on summer Sundays. She loved that the church was right on the harbor front and added a colorful new stained-glass window almost every year, unlike her much plainer church in Worcester.

After helping transport her satchels and belongings to the little room under the eaves she would share with Nan, Fannie sped to her mother.

"Please may I run down to the river?" she begged. "Just to say hello and see if my favorite great blue heron is there? Please?"

Her mother sighed, "Oh, alright Fannie, but let your sister come along." Ethel was eight. Susan Perkins was likely grateful for a quiet break after the long day traveling with her daughters, one a bundle of energy, impatience, and questions, the other inclined to pout and complain.

Fannie didn't walk to the river; she ran, with Ethel behind her, whining and struggling to keep up. The lane was winding, and bumpy with tree roots, but she felt nimble-footed in her sturdy lace-up shoes, and the path was a familiar friend. Past the big boulders, old stone fences, fields, and evergreens she flew. And suddenly, there it was, a beautiful pale green highway of water, and a small, picture-perfect cove, its wharf stretching out into the river. The sisters made their way along the shore toward a view of the harbor and village, less than two miles upstream. Her great blue heron was hiding. But she knew he'd be back when the tide was right to wade for his supper. It was a special treat to watch him slowly, patiently pick his way along on spindly legs, his slender neck bobbing with each step, and then his beak darting down to catch a fish. Now *that* was a sight one didn't get to see in Worcester!

She planned to pepper her parents this very night with questions about what day trips they could look forward to in the weeks ahead. Perhaps they'd celebrate the Fourth of July in town and see fireworks from The Bridge! Maybe her parents would agree to have the wagon take them up Bunker Hill to spread a picnic on her favorite hilltop, with the view of the big, long, lake called Damariscotta Pond. Now that she was twelve, she was determined to excel at all evening parlor games.

Dreamily wandering back to the house, she tried to guess how soon Grandma Perkins would bid her to lie flat on her back on the biggest table and pile a few heavy books on her chest. That would mean it was time for Fannie's lessons in elocution: loudly and clearly projecting her voice. Somehow Grandma Perkins, her favorite confidant and source of gentle guidance, seemed to understand her better than anyone in the whole world. She apparently somehow knew that Fannie would one day have big crowds to address, eager to hear her every word.

No wonder Frances, born Fannie Coralie Perkins, would come back to this place throughout her entire life. It was her special, nearly sacred, refuge from the world. Whenever she thought or spoke of her one true home, wherever else she resided, it was The Brick House in Newcastle, Maine.

Chapter 3: Family and Foundations

Growing Up

It was a Massachusetts childhood. She was born in Boston in 1880, but from the age of two, Frances was raised in the city of Worcester, (pronounced "Wooster") where her father owned a stationery and business supply store. Her parents moved there, about forty miles to the west of Boston, because her father felt his business would do better in Worcester.

A photographer captured the Perkins's first child at age four looking quite angelic with long golden curls, a sweet solemn face, and serious round eyes.

She was named and baptized Fannie Coralie Perkins. Later on, she would change her name from Fannie (which the family often spelled Fanny) to just Frances. Perhaps she sensed that it would be easier to be taken seriously as "Frances" than as "Fanny." Or she may have thought her given name too old-fashioned. The boy's name Francis *sounds* just like the girl's name Frances. Possibly she felt a male-sounding name would help her make something of herself in a man's world.

But the most logical explanation is that when she was confirmed into the new church denomination she chose at age twenty-five, she was asked to select a confirmation name. She chose Frances, and soon made it her legal name. She was to keep her maiden name, Perkins, for the rest of her life.

Family Dynamics

Fannie grew up in a warm, nurturing family. She had a happy, harmonious relationship with both her parents. Her only sibling, Ethel, four years younger, was another matter. She was given to tantrums when she didn't get her way!

It was a typical dinnertime in the Perkins household. Papa liked to use the evening meal to discuss current events or teach his daughters something new and interesting. But his plan often failed. One night, little Ethel flounced down in her chair clearly out of sorts and demanded, "What are we having for dinner?"

"Pork chops, dear, mashed potatoes, and peas," her mother calmly replied.

"NO!" shouted Ethel, pushing her chair backward so abruptly it fell over. "We have pork chops all the time, and you know I hate peas! They're horrible. I won't eat them! I won't."

Exchanging worried looks, both parents attempted to soothe Ethel, and asked her to pick up her chair. Instead, she burst into furious tears, swept her entire place setting onto the floor, shattering her plate, and ran from the room.

On many occasions Ethel, when crossed or corrected, created even worse household havoc. It was unusually difficult for her to accept that she couldn't always have her own way. She knew that good behavior was expected of her, but only learned very slowly, over a span of years, how to control her temper. In the end, Fannie admired Ethel's success. She would be often reminded of her sibling many years later when grown men in Albany or Washington, or on the site of labor negotiations, blustered, pounded the table, or shouted. She always felt that the Ethel experience helped her deal with adult tantrums, and put them in a different perspective. An outburst did not faze or intimidate her. Her thinking was that if a young girl could learn to contain her temper, why not a grown man?

It was an ordinary, conventional, and rather conservative upbringing. Her parents were solidly Republican and were equally staunch Congregationalists. New England was a section of the country that always prized itself on its "Yankee values" of thrift, honesty, hard work, practicality, self-reliance, and a reserved manner. Most New Englanders of their day were law-abiding, faithful church-goers, and disapproved of complaining or displaying emotions, especially in public. They tended to be private about personal feelings. They were strong believers in democracy. Frances absorbed and lived up to those standards, engrained in her at an early age.

Her mother, Susan Bean Perkins, had an excellent sense of humor, and could be fun. She had a particular flair for drawing, entertaining her daughters and neighborhood children with her amusing art work. One summer day Fannie and Ethel brought a few of the neighborhood children in for a glass of their mother's delicious homemade lemonade. Mrs. Perkins surprised them all by coming into the kitchen with her drawing pad and pencils, and announcing, "What shall I draw for each of you? What's your favorite animal?," she asked of the youngest child first. The children gathered around and watched in wide-eyed delight as first a beagle, and then in rapid succession, per each request, a giraffe, and elephant, a moose, and a tarantula emerged. Each was whimsical, and each child ran home with a drawing to show off. When the same troop of children clamored for more a couple of weeks later, Mrs. Perkins was prepared with modeling clay. Soon she had a parade of little animals and people marching across the table.

And Susan Bean Perkins was a woman who always spoke her mind. A cousin described her as "not bashful about expressing her ideas." Also, significantly, she was a generous, caring person. If a relative needed help, she was there to lend a hand. And her generosity extended to the wider community. She and her husband volunteered time through their church for charity work, outreach, and assistance to people in need. Sometimes the Perkins would even help another family with their rent. Mrs. Perkins' example taught her daughters the importance of caring for those less fortunate.

Her father, though not a college graduate, was a man who loved learning. He was, in fact, a classical scholar. He had pushed himself to learn Greek and Latin, often reading ancient poetry, speeches, and plays in their original language. When Fannie was small, he would entertain her with stories from Greek mythology, sometimes at the dinner table. It was common for him to announce a topic while the family finished the meal. "Tonight, you girls will learn something about the Civil War," for instance. He also liked geography, the study of law, and discussing politics, among many other topics. In him Frances had another great role model. He soon saw the unusual intelligence of his eldest daughter. One day when she was just eight, he called her to his big desk and asked, "Fannie, how would you like to learn to read a bit of Greek?"

She tilted her head, thought, and replied, "Well, Papa, I think I would like to try." They dove right in, and she proved a quick student with a fine memory. After the first attempt, Fannie couldn't get enough of Greek lessons with Papa. It was an opportunity to have him all to herself, and have his full attention.

Her father discussed politics and world events with her regularly. By age fourteen, ready to leave grammar school and head for Worcester Classical High School, she was well prepared.

Child rearing in the late 1800s when she was growing up was considerably different than in the average American home today. Most parents then believed that "children should be seen and not heard." This may have been what led her father to put a stop to his very verbal child's tendency to chatter on and on. She was talking at length about her classmates one day, and describing in detail a little play their teacher was letting them put on in class. Exasperated, he spoke up firmly, interrupting her. "Fannie! If you have anything to say, say it definitely, and stop." The admonishment stung for a moment. But she never forgot that advice.

Few nineteenth century parents spoiled, coddled, or catered to their children, who were expected to help out or do chores and then left to entertain themselves. Many parents believed in the Biblical advice, "spare the rod and spoil the child." That meant that corporal punishment such as spankings or whippings, including in the school room, were common.

The Shopping Trip

There is no evidence that either Perkins parent spanked their daughters. But neither would they ever think to pay one a compliment on her appearance, behavior, or talents. That was considered to lead to a vain or conceited child. On the contrary, Fannie well remembered her mother's almost brutally frank assessment of her looks on a shopping trip to Boston when she was about twelve.

For most of Frances's life, no lady of any age would leave her home without her hat on. One day her mother announced, "It's time to go find you a new hat, Fannie. You old one is too small, and looking a bit bedraggled." So off they went.

When her mother picked out a certain one and said, "THAT is your hat!" well, that was that! It was a tricorn, or three-pointed, hat not unlike the ones worn by the revolutionary war patriots and founding fathers, though smaller.

One of the Perkins ancestors, a colonial leader and patriot at the time of the American Revolution, was James Otis, Jr. Learning all about this proud forebear in her family history made Fannie proud too. She had been hearing tales of James

Otis and his sister, Mercy Otis, both noted for their fierce independence, for as long as she could remember. So, when given a little tricorn as a ten-year-old, she delighted in it, and wore it often. This may have softened the blow of her mother's decree, though the words she used were blunt and unflattering: "You have a very broad face. Your head is actually narrower above the temples than it is at the cheek-bones. Also, it slopes off very suddenly into your chin.... never let yourself get a hat that is narrower than your cheekbones, because it makes you look ridiculous."

Many young girls would have withered or wept under such a critique, but apparently Frances took her mother's words to heart. For the rest of her life, she was seldom seen in public without her trademark tricorn, or a hat of a similar style.

It is significant that Frances had not one, but two heroic colonial patriots in her family tree. James Otis, Jr. is credited with saying "Taxation without representation is tyranny," and was a fiery orator, speaking out against British policies as early as 1761. When he made a five-hour speech in the legislature defending American liberty, John Adams wrote, "American Independence was then and there born." When Otis's health failed, his sister, Mercy Otis, took up the patriot mantle, which of course was highly unusual for a woman in the colonial era. Mercy organized political meetings and wrote and published regular satires, poems, and plays attacking the British. She was one of the first women ever to write for the public in America and instrumental in organizing the critically important Committees of Correspondence between the colonies in the pre-Revolutionary period. Both her mother and grandmother frequently shared this family lore, relating stories of the Otis line going back to both the American Revolution and the French and Indian war.

So Fannie was born with the blood of two patriotic ancestors running in her veins, one of them a woman. She grew up knowing that one person could help change the world by bravely speaking truth to power, even at the risk of life and limb.

A First Lesson in Poverty

Always a curious child, Fannie came home perplexed one day. She had questions for her parents. At dinner she announced, "I have a friend at school who always dresses in shabby, nearly outgrown clothes — and she has just a few of them." That day she had visited the girl's home and was shocked. Clearly the family was quite poor. Her friend and her siblings were very thin. "Papa, their little house looked so rickety! And Sarah told me the roof leaks whenever it rains hard. Why are some people so much poorer than our family?"

"Well, my dear," responded her father slowly, "people tend to become poor if they don't work hard enough."

"Or if the parents spend their money on liquor," added her mother primly.

This thinking was a standard misconception about society in that day and age; her parents were not alone. But it made Fannie curious. She knew both of her friend's parents worked hard, her father in a textile mill, and her mother raising four children, tending a garden, chopping wood, cooking and cleaning. She saw no sign of drinking in their home. And so she wondered.

School Days

As a girl, Fannie did not apply herself diligently to all her studies. She never excelled or led her class. She relied instead on her natural quickness to catch on to concepts without study. She trusted that her verbal gifts could make up for any shortcomings in her exams and essays. Her interests and strengths lay in the arts, history, speaking, reading and writing.

But she *was* a star on the debate team, which, like her whole high school, was made up mostly of boys. After one debate, which her side resoundingly won, she was gathering up her notes when a boy from the opposing side approached her shyly and awkwardly, but with wide eyes. He blurted out, "Gee, Fannie, you sure know how to argue a point. I don't know how you come up with ideas and words so... *fast!*" The young man apparently had never before met a girl with fine logic and extensive verbal skills. He seemed astonished by the idea that a girl's thinking could match a boy's. Fannie blushed at the compliment and mumbled "thank you" before turning away. Undoubtedly debating helped her develop skill in thinking quickly and speaking persuasively. And clearly the academic skills she developed at her city's public college prep school, Worcester Classical High School, laid a solid educational foundation for her future.

Her approach to school worked well enough to get by in high school. Upon graduation, the next logical step was enrolling in higher education. Her father had long expected that she would go to college, though at the time only three percent of women went on for studies after high school. Fewer than one in four college students were female, and only a tiny percent of Americans went to college at all, unlike today. In fact, early in the 1900's only about ten percent of people graduated from high school!

But Fannie's mother was already making a list of "suitable" young men, or "suitors." In that era, it was common for women to marry while still in their teens. Mrs. Perkins would have liked her daughter to find a husband sooner rather than later. Her father, on the other hand, spoke decisively, and often repeated, "Our daughter would make a fine teacher. Fannie, you have a good mind. College should be your next step." And she was eager to learn all she could.

Fannie chose an excellent college for women in South Hadley, Massachusetts, about fifty miles away, an easy train trip from home. It was Mount Holyoke, founded in 1837. She was in for her first real challenge. And it was to come as a shock.

Chapter 4

Perk Emerges

COLLEGE! Fun, Friends, and Freedom? Or Frustration, Floundering, and Fear of Failure? For the future Frances Perkins, the answer was a mixture of all of the above.

She loved Mount Holyoke College right from the start. It was a lushly beautiful campus surrounded by rolling hills, and boasted a stream, lakes, a dam and an old stone mill. There were woods around the campus with its handsome classical buildings of brick and stone. The little village green, with a fountain and Civil War memorial statue, was opposite the campus. Fannie found it all an idyllic retreat from Worcester.

She eagerly tried out the newly popular game of basketball, which the girls played in bloomers, but found that indoor sports were not one of her strengths. During her second semester a new friend approached her. "Fannie, there are auditions next week for the spring play. Will you come with me? You know, for moral support. But you should try for a role too. You have such a good strong voice." Fannie thought for a long moment, then said, "Why not? It sounds like it could be fun." This was an opportunity she hadn't had at Worcester Classical High. She was apparently bitten by the theater bug in her first play. Acting quickly became her favorite activity outside the classroom. In one student production she played Brutus in Shakespeare's tragedy, *Julius Caesar*, a major role. She took on numerous roles during her college years, relishing acting so much that for a time she considered a stage career.

She whole-heartedly embraced the spiritual mission of the school, "to live for God and do something." The founder, Mary Lyon, had originally launched the college as a "Female Seminary," with a strong emphasis on religion. Her motto was "Go forward, attempt great things, accomplish great things." Frances Perkins was destined to live out that motto more than any other graduate of the college before or since. She firmly believed that being religious meant that she had a duty to help others. She just didn't yet know how she would do that.

Fannie didn't object to the required household chores, almost an hour a day. She didn't mind the regular attendance at church services expected. Religion appealed to her, particularly the idea that good works were important and that Christian teachings were to be acted on.

Fannie's personality blossomed in college. She had been painfully shy as a child, once admitting she found it a struggle to even approach a librarian for a book, or to enter a shop and ask for a spool of thread. She'd had few close childhood friends. Now she developed a reputation as a great talker, unusually articulate, a bit of a joker, and a master kite flyer. She was also known as something of a non-conformist, often breaking the rule on "lights out" in order to stay awake talking with a friend or two. Her popularity grew, and along with it came a new nickname: "Perk." Or sometimes, "Perky."

It began when she sat one late fall evening with a group of other girls living in her dorm. Fannie was making them all laugh: "It's a good thing that I was rubbish on the basketball court. I looked like a cow overdue for her milking in those bloomers!" As the laughter died down, the girl who had collapsed backward onto her bed in giggles sat up and said, "Oh Fannie, you are the life of the party — the perkiest one in the class. I hereby christen you 'Perk!'" The others chimed in with their approval, and the nickname was destined to stick for four years.

Problems, however, quickly emerged in her classwork. Her freshman year Latin class made her, she said, "for the first time… conscious of character." In high school she had passed with ease by giving translations that she considered close enough. But at Mount Holyoke, that approach was not good enough. Her professor recognized her bluffing, and demanded exact translations. From that teacher she learned what real academic work was and how one handled it.

Hurdles

Her sophomore year held still greater challenges. Not until the third year could students choose their courses; the first two years were full of course requirements. Her biggest hurdle was chemistry, not a subject she would have chosen, being drawn more to history and literature. She had not had much background or preparation in the sciences.

Perk found herself floundering, and wondered if she'd even pass the course. But this professor too detected Fannie's intelligence and "hounded" her to rise to the challenge. And so she did. Success was not achieved without tears of sheer frustration! Nevertheless, she persisted. She'd decided to prove to herself that despite the difficulty, she could master the material. Here's how she remembered it: "My intellectual pride was aroused and the grim determination awakened in me to get the most I could out of college." She added, "I discovered for the first time, under the stimulus of that course and of that teacher, that I had a mind." She had no regrets about her experience with "Dr. Goldthwaite's hounding personality, and the pounding impact of her intelligence." Later as a teacher, Fannie would carry the inspiration that teacher gave her forward, telling her students to "avoid snap courses, and welcome mental discipline." In the end, that chemistry teacher became her faculty adviser, and Fannie chose chemistry as her major with minors in physics and biology.

During her college years Perk's leadership qualities developed and she and her classmates grew close. By her junior year they elected her to be class vice president. She headed the campus YWCA. She came up with the idea for a very creative and successful class fundraiser, a mid-morning sandwich sale, which continued long after she graduated. As a senior, she was elected "Class President for Life."

Senior Year Sparks

Fannie was beginning to evolve and mature in college as she was exposed to new ideas. She later recalled, "like many young people, I was an ardent fan of President Theodore Roosevelt." She was impressed by his "progressive ideas." She liked his stand that all Americans deserved a "Square Deal," not just big business owners. She agreed with the president that there had to be better opportunities for working people and that conditions in the country's cities had to improve.

As Perk's last year at Mount Holyoke began, she couldn't know that two events would soon have an even greater influence. Both lit major sparks in her, influencing who she would become and what she would do with her life.

Meeting a Legend

The first event was the visit to Mount Holyoke of a woman named Florence Kelley. Fannie had attended several meetings of the campus chapter of an organization called the National Consumers' League. The League's purpose was to educate the public about horrific working conditions in the country at that time, especially the horrors of child labor and tenement sweatshops. The League was determined to do away with both.

The League had sent their top speaker, Kelley, to the college. She was a dynamic, independent woman sometimes described as a "raging furnace." In a letter to a friend Perk wrote that the speech "first opened my mind to the necessity for the work that became my vocation."

Kelley was a fiery crusader for social justice. Her speeches were dramatic and emotional. She would, for example, describe young boys who were laboring in glass blowing factories. She would paint a verbal picture of them running back and forth to red hot ovens, being kicked and called "dogs" as they were ordered about. She would make audiences "see" and feel their suffering. Fannie was at once inflamed and inspired. She began to see that she must devote her life to helping overturn such practices as child labor.

Her path was to cross Florence Kelley's many, many times in years to come. At Kelley's funeral thirty years after they had first met, Frances Perkins eulogized her role model, saying, "She took a whole group of young people, formless… and molded their aspirations for social justice into some definite purpose."

Field Trips: A Wake-Up Call

Also that year, Fannie went on outings away from campus. They were an astonishing revelation. Her American Economic History professor had a revolutionary approach to opening her students' eyes to the real world. She took them to the nearby paper factories and textile mills of Holyoke, Massachusetts. The students were not meant to simply visit, but inspect, ask questions, and write reports on the conditions they found. Fannie wrote, "I was astonished and fascinated by what I saw."

In the late 1800's, the Industrial Revolution had arrived, with mills and factories springing up like mushrooms after the rain, all over New England and elsewhere. Most were grim, dark, brick buildings, poorly lit and even more poorly ventilated. And they could be death traps. Safety was of little concern to employers and management bosses consumed only with making a profit.

In the clothing industries, factory owners mostly employed young women, often teenagers. Many of them were newly arrived in the country, or had migrated from the south to the cities of the north for employment. Sadly, the workers included a great number of children, sometimes as young as five. Factory owners liked to hire women, immigrants, and children because those workers were so desperate. They would work long hours for pennies a day. In contrast to today's typical eight-hour work day, they labored twelve or even fourteen hours. That meant that in winter, they arrived before it was fully light, and left after dark, seldom seeing the light of day. Almost all had to work on Saturdays, and frequently even on Sundays. If one told the boss that there were laws preventing labor on the Sabbath, she would be fired.

No wonder the students, who were well-bred, well-fed young women at a topnotch college, were shocked and horrified by what they saw. At least, Fannie was. She had to write summaries of what she witnessed, and grew outraged by the dirt, dangerous conditions, and lack of light and air; and the children, who should have been in school instead of laboring in mills. Fannie was so appalled that the experience changed her. It began to turn her into a person who was passionate about reforming such conditions.

She recalled her parents' opinion that poverty was due to laziness or drinking. But after seeing the factories and mills, Fannie felt that they "opened the door to the idea" that there were other causes that made people poor.

Fannie graduated in 1902. At her graduation she gave a speech, using as her text a passage from the Bible, 1 Corinthians 15:58, the source of the words the class had chosen as its motto, "Be Ye Stedfast" (unwavering), an echo of the college's mission statement. She would remain so for life.

She was not at the top academically but had been voted the student who had done the most for her class. And she was a much-changed young woman from the eighteen-year-old who had entered Mount Holyoke in 1898. Their class motto echoed in her; but she was not yet fully formed in her resolve to tackle the world and change it. It wasn't going to be easy.

Let's take a look at the world into which she was about to be launched.

Chapter 5

Portrait of an Era

Life in the U.S. in the early 20th century was of course very different. Still, some things may surprise you.

Some Firsts and Fun Facts From 1902:

- *The Tale of Peter Rabbit* by Beatrix Potter was first published.

- Teddy bears became wildly popular. They were named after the President, Theodore Roosevelt. Though an avid hunter, he once spared the mother of a small bear cub, so his name became associated with the bear.

- Crayola Crayons debuted in stores.

- The first airplane flight was a year away. Orville and Wilbur Wright were working on realizing their dream.

Not so comfortingly familiar were the hard facts of life in America.

The Way We Were in 1902:

- The population of the entire U.S. was 79 million; today it is about 335 million.

- Being illiterate was common.

- Only one in ten children reaching high school age could read. Why? Most spent their days laboring on farms, in factories, and in coal mines. Little money was spent on public education. Less than one in ten of those who attended school graduated from high school.

- The average life span was just age 48 for whites, and only 33 years for black Americans.

- Most people did not own a bathtub. Indoor plumbing was rare. Thus, many people only washed their hair once or twice a month.

- Many women had ten, twelve, or more children, as birth control was almost non-existent. Condoms and diaphragms to prevent pregnancy were developed in the 1800's, but the Comstock Law of 1873 made it a federal crime to sell or distribute them.

- Almost all babies were born at home, not in hospitals. Hospitals were considered dangerous due to the very high risk of infection.

- It was then thirty times more dangerous to go to work, as so many workplace conditions were unsafe.

- Most elementary school teachers were women, because it was legal to pay them much less than men. High school jobs were traditionally reserved for men.

- Typewriters, trains, and skyscrapers were new, and the first overseas phone call had been made in 1900. But indoor plumbing for toilets, tubs, and sinks was still on the horizon for most people. Movies were just being born, first with "views" lasting just a few seconds.

- Automobiles, originally called horseless carriages, were brand new. Henry Ford had not yet begun producing them on his famous assembly line, so almost no one had a car. There were only a dozen or so miles of paved roads to drive them on!

- The industrial revolution had led to great wealth and leisure for some, poverty and loss of hope for others. Big business tycoons were making fortunes, becoming richer than kings. But factory and mine workers slaved for much less than a dollar a day.

What Was a Woman's Life Like Then?

To fully appreciate the enormity of what Frances Perkins did in her lifetime, you first need to have a clear picture of what the world was like for middle-class women in her day. Here are some facts:

- No woman had ever served in Congress.

- Women could not serve on juries.

- Married women could not hold property, get credit or a loan, or even have a bank account in their own name.

- Women could not be admitted to the top Ivy League Colleges such as Harvard, Yale and Princeton. With the exception of Cornell, the "Ivies" did not open their doors to women until the late *1970's*!

- Women were also barred from the nation's top law schools and medical schools.

- The American Bar Association for lawyers, and the American Medical Association for doctors both refused women members.

- Women could not serve as clergy, serve in the armed forces, or enter most professions and occupations. Most employed women worked as domestic servants — maids, cooks, and nannies — nurses, or lower school teachers, if lucky enough to find work outside of a mill or factory.

- Women could not vote except in a few western states, and in local elections in some places, though the fight for suffrage had been waged since the 1860's.

Only ten percent of American women remained single. But among female college graduates, the figure was inching toward fifty percent.

A-ha! With that last statistic, we're getting closer to how the role of women in society was slowly changing. The fortunate few who received a higher education were beginning to challenge the ideal of womanhood that had existed in society for a very long time. They were seeing in themselves a new identity as people, equal to men, with the ability to remain self-sufficient. They were ground-breakers.

Of course, to ensure survival, poorer women had always worked long, hard hours. But in Frances's day people still expected a middle-class woman's first responsibility to be within the home, devoting her life to domestic routines. Anything else was thought to lead to a loss of morals in society. In other words, public opinion was stacked against a woman who strayed from the old, traditional ideal that a woman should marry. If she didn't, she was considered a "spinster," or "old maid," doomed to be dependent on others.

Against this background, in these times, what chance did a bright, dedicated, and idealistic young woman stand? We shall see.

Chapter 6

Just Getting Started

There was destined to be a certain amount of friction in the Perkins household when the new college graduate didn't return home right away. After all, there's bound to be conflict when a parent's view of the proper path forward differs from that of their offspring! Fannie was burning to help the poor in some way, to "do something!" And so, against her parents' wishes, she decided to take the train to New York City. She wanted to see if she could find some type of social work. In urgent posts her parents tried to talk her out of it. Her father protested that the city was a "den of iniquity." She was unswayed.

First Job Interview

Fannie found her way to the New York office of the Charity Organization Society, which would later on become the United Way. She was young — just 22 — and without experience. Nonetheless, she recounted, she went in without an appointment and "demanding to see Mr. Devine, whose name I knew." He was the director. She knew that with her full cheeks, tapering down to a small, pointed chin, she looked very young. She later wrote of having a "round face, wide-eyed look that makes you look even younger than you really are. I actually did have my hair up to look older". In college she had worn it in a braid down her back. Still, she later admitted, "If anyone had said I was fifteen, no one would have disputed it." Nevertheless, she boldly insisted she would meet only with the director. Finally, he agreed. Their interview went something like this:

"Mr. Devine, my purpose here is to ask for a position with the Charity Society."

"And what do you think you'd like to do here, Miss Perkins?"

"I understand you have workers who visit poor families who need relief, give them food, and help unravel their problems. I'd like to do that sort of work."

A strange smile played across Mr. Devine's lips. He replied after a moment, "Well, that's very interesting! Tell me: suppose you were sent out to visit a family who had applied for help, and when you entered their tenement room, you found the father drunk on the bed, the children sick with sore throats, with no food in the house, the dirty dishes piled high in the sink, and the drunken father having obviously just beaten his wife? What would you do?"

Fannie promptly said, "Why, I'd send for the police and have that man arrested, of course."

The smile widened on the director's face and he replied, "That isn't exactly what *we* would recommend." Though her heart was in the right place, clearly Fannie had failed the test.

In the minutes that followed, Mr. Devine went on to explain that rehabilitation consisted of getting parents to work, to stay sober, and fulfill their responsibilities. He also explained that no one so young would be hired for such a position because she hadn't enough experience of life to have good judgment about what to do for the poor and needy.

Humbled, Fannie asked his advice on what to do to prepare herself. He said, "Why not get yourself a job teaching? The passing of some years, combined with what you read and observe will give you some experience." He went on to recommend a few books, and sent her away with a handful of the Charity Society's bulletins to read.

One of his recommendations had an enormous impact on her. It was a book about what life was really like for the poor living in tenement buildings in New York City. It was called *How the Other Half Lives*, by Jacob Riis. It opened her eyes to how fortunate and sheltered she was, and she was "deeply moved" by its descriptions of want and need.

Back In Worcester

And so Fannie came home. Her parents (or at least her mother) encouraged her to look for a husband, and discouraged graduate school studies, a path she would have liked to pursue. Her father, from the start, had suggested she teach. She relented, and at first took on short assignments as a science teacher at a few secondary schools in Worcester and beyond. Her students liked her and found her energetic, fun — and very fashionable. While at home, she taught Sunday school and took part in activities at her church.

For years she had read about Hull House, the famous settlement house in Chicago founded by Jane Addams. Settlement houses helped struggling workers, the poor, and immigrants by recruiting college graduates as volunteers. Education and self-improvement for the poor were stressed. They opened nurseries and kindergartens at the settlement houses, as well as clubs for boys and girls. They fed people who needed a meal. They dispensed advice.

The Girls' Club

Fannie took the idea of starting a girls' club from what she had read about Hull House. At a settlement house in Worcester, she invited fourteen- to sixteen-year-old girls to join. But they were not in high school. They were mostly factory and millworkers or shop girls, under-fed and under-paid. They also suffered from a lack of exercise, so Fannie organized games, sports, and outings for them. She presented some educational programs. When she found they liked to sing, she brought them new songs. She was rehearsing them for a singing performance, a fundraiser so they could buy a basketball.

Then the unthinkable happened. One of the teenagers, a worker in a candy factory, had her hand cut off in a candy dipper.

Fannie visited the girl in her home and promptly sent for a doctor. She may have had to pay the doctor herself. The factory had simply sent the girl home. It came as a shock that the candy factory had no legal responsibility to make any payment to a seriously injured worker. Desperate, Fannie appealed to a clergyman she knew. Together they approached the employer. Their joint plea persuaded the factory owner to make a small, one-time award of $100. Had it not been for Fannie, the maimed teenager would not have received a cent for the loss of her hand.

Moving On

Before two years in Worcester were up, she learned that there was an opening in the science department at a women's college in a suburb of Chicago. She grabbed it, sight unseen. *Beyond* eager to leave Worcester and the constrictions of family life, Fannie struck out for Chicago, where her new life in social work was to truly begin.

Chapter 7

Developing Determination

Teaching, Learning, Growing, Changing

The great city of Chicago was bound to be an awakening in many ways for a young person from New England. Her new job was at a prominent boarding school for girls called Ferry Hall in the Chicago suburb of Lake Forest. There she taught both biology and physics and headed a dormitory. For three years she was successful and popular. Her students there described her as imaginative and witty. But when she left her position at the end of those three years she was headed for a very different career. You could certainly say she "took the path less traveled by." And that made all the difference. It was to be half a century before she re-entered teaching, as a guest college professor. The years as a Ferry Hall science teacher were overshadowed by major changes in Fannie's life. In June of 1905, exactly three years after her college graduation, she changed both her name and her religion.

New Church, New Name

She had been baptized a Protestant and raised in her parents' Congregational faith, but came to find the Episcopal church more to her liking. The more formal and structured services there appealed to her, and their elaborate rituals made her feel calmer in a stressful world. Even the formal, Gothic-inspired look of the church, compared to the stark simplicity of a New England Protestant church, was to her liking. Some described this branch of the Episcopal Church as Anglo-Catholic, as it was in some ways akin to Catholicism, a religion she had also considered. When she mentioned her thoughts of becoming a Roman Catholic to her parents, they nearly had a stroke. The Episcopal denomination was, at least, a branch of Protestantism.

But Fannie was an adult now and had grown independent. Above all, she felt drawn to her new church's emphasis on a more just social order. She liked their commitment to helping the poor. The Episcopal church had become affiliated with the labor movement, with which she was impressed: she could see how significantly it helped change people's lives.

Changing faiths meant being re-confirmed. As part of an ancient tradition, akin to a "coming of age" ritual, the person being confirmed was asked to choose a new name, a symbol of her now taking charge of her life. She chose Frances, and decided that her confirmation name would be the one she'd use exclusively from then on.

The Settlement Worker

Frances had another major focus during her teaching years. It was her volunteer work in the settlement houses of Chicago. Two of the most famous ones in the country were there: Hull House and Chicago Commons. There she met people in the labor movement who also wanted to improve conditions and wages for workers. Some of them were Episcopalians or Anglo-Catholics.

The settlement houses were all located in city slums. They depended on people — most of them young, well-educated volunteers — to help poor people improve their lives through assistance, education, and creating a sense of community. Settlement houses were popping up in American cities starting in the 1890's. Their number doubled between 1900 and 1910, patterned on the successful British model of Toynbee Hall, founded by students at Oxford University. A professor there named John Ruskin had argued for programs to make life livable for the throngs of people that the Industrial Revolution had made poor. Ruskin wanted better housing for workers. He talked about such programs as a system of social security, creating jobs through employment on public works, and passing laws requiring that a minimum wage be paid. He placed emphasis on better education.

But these ideas were only in their infancy in America. Here the emphasis was on reforms such as better sanitation and building parks. Chicago Commons had merged with older church and synagogue charities to better meet the great demand by the time Frances arrived on the scene.

Just imagine the overwhelming feelings of a young, middle-class woman trying to make a difference in the lives of people who lived in overcrowded, poorly built slum housing, wore ragged clothes, and suffered from poor diet and diseases.

As she became immersed in their lives, she grew greatly discomforted. She had a secure job in a prestigious private school, a fashionable wardrobe, and a little money to shop or go to plays and concerts in Chicago. But people living nearby couldn't properly feed or clothe their children. They lived in unhealthy and dangerously unsafe tenement apartments. She concluded, "I had to do something about unnecessary hazards... unnecessary poverty. It was sort of up to me. This feeling... sprang out of a period of great philosophical confusion." Some of the confusion stemmed from a part of her wanting an easier life, perhaps a career in the arts, writing, drawing, or acting. But there was constantly a pull in the other direction from her conscience and her strong desire to be a part of righting great wrongs.

Learning that the Democratic Party was more committed to helping solve the problems of the poor, she announced to her family, who were staunch Republicans, that she was now a Democrat. Again, they were shocked. Of course, she was really only announcing her allegiance to a philosophy, as women could not vote.

When Christmas break of 1905 arrived, instead of going home to attend parties and catch up with old friends, she went to live at the Chicago Commons settlement house as a "temporary resident." There were many work opportunities there: nursing sick people, arguing employers into paying what they owed workers, and raising funds for the settlement house.

Facts Feed Anger; Anger Feeds Determination

Once Frances learned more about Chicago, she was stunned and angry. She found that out of about 50,000 people working in the clothing industry, three out of four were immigrants, of which half were women and girls. They were being paid only two or three dollars a week at a time when a living wage was considered eight dollars. It was shocking to learn how long their hours were, and how appalling their work conditions. She learned that unemployed people faced despair, panic, and sickness, often followed by death.

One day a person at Hull House referred to "the bundle women." "Why are they called that?" she asked.

"Because they carry bundles of piece work home to sew, of course," her co-worker replied. "They are paid not by the hour, but by the piece." The next night she noticed on the street near a mill that people from the settlement house were handing out small bottles of milk to women carrying bundles home. Again, being naïve, Frances asked why. She was told, "Oh, it's common. We regularly donate it to people with children in the family." Frances was shocked. "Are people so poor that their babies die for lack of food?" she cried.

Frances quickly learned that, as she put it, "The lower classes don't sit around and pity themselves." They were up and going and trying to get somewhere. She met and spoke with two cheerful immigrant girls who worked in a clothing factory and shared a basement room. They each made at most five dollars a week, paid by the piece sewn. They told Frances they paid $2.50 weekly for the room. Trying to help them with their budget, Frances asked, "If you pay two-fifty for the rent, how much do you use for food and what do you eat?" They laughed, and in broken English told her, "Oh, we've discovered what to eat. We mostly eat bread and bananas. It fills you up so you don't feel hungry at all." Imagine living on that diet.

At a social gathering of settlement house volunteers, she vented her outrage, saying: "How can we cure this? Is it to go on forever, these people being so poor that we have to give out free milk and nursing services, the babies die, there's nothing to do on a Sunday afternoon but get drunk? What *can* be done?" A co-worker about her own age, but far more experienced, told her the only answer was to organize trade unions. "Absolutely," he said. "If every working man and woman would join a trade union then the wages would be sufficient to support people, and then the families would be able to look after themselves," without the need for charities or settlement houses. When she was still skeptical, he pointed out that construction workers like bricklayers, carpenters, and plumbers had unions and were far better off. There were no unions for people who worked in mills and the clothing industry. And women were paid only half of what men were, even in those jobs.

Frances Warms to Unions

The importance of unions was a new idea to Frances. Back at home in Worcester, they were often considered at best, suspect, and at worst, a negative or shady enterprise. But ever curious and eager to learn, she began to attend union lectures and organizational meetings. When she went to a meeting of the bookbinders' union, she came away impressed that this union had always admitted women, and one was even vice president! At a meeting of the printers' union, she learned that though there were women printers, the union refused them membership. But she also learned that those women were better off simply because there was a union in place for their trade.

When her Christmas break "vacation" was over, she wrote in her class letter to her Mount Holyoke classmates, "I never got so many ideas in my life as I did in those three weeks!" And Frances was decidedly developing determination along with ideas. After that she spent all her vacations, as well as every weekend possible, at one of the settlement houses, taking on various tasks. One was to accompany a district nurse on rounds to sick and desperate families. Some situations were just as her interviewer in New York had described a few years earlier, with sickness, drunkenness, crying children and dirty conditions common. In one tenement, in order to wash the entire family, she and the nurse had to make numerous trips down the street to a fire hydrant, as there was no running water. On another assignment, at a home in which the mother was very ill, the nurse told Frances, "For heaven's sake, wash up the dishes, and then wash up the children." This required heating water on a little gas stove after inserting coins from her pocket. "Now wash up Father." This was made very challenging due to his vomiting from being drunk!

Another challenge she took on was trying to collect wages for workers. For instance, women would do what was called piecework in a "sweatshop," usually either a dark, airless basement or their own tenement room. On returning finished goods, say, blouses with seams sewn, hems finished, and buttons added, the employer would accept the work and then refuse to pay. Sometimes a worker was owed weeks of pay. An immigrant woman was easy to cheat, as she didn't have the money, time, or command of English to go to court. Enter Frances. Again, her training was scant, but she used her wits. When one employer refused to pay back wages, she replied, "Well then. I will report to your landlord that you, and the shop you are running, are dishonest, and cheat people!" The statement was simply an idea that just popped into her head. But it worked, so after that, the line was a useful tool in her arsenal.

On To Philadelphia

Having made up her mind to leave teaching and become a social worker, she wrote to everyone she could think of who had a connection that might lead to a job with a charity or a reform organization. Finally, a girlfriend in Boston wrote that there was a job opening in Philadelphia, Pennsylvania, with their Research and Protective Association, formed by concerned citizens to investigate some terrible practices in that city. Young girls arriving as immigrants from Europe, and young black women from the South, were being preyed on by thieves, pimps, and employers eager to exploit their labor in exchange for rock bottom wages. Frances applied and was promptly hired — for fifty dollars a month, less than she had been paid teaching. She pawned her watch so she would not have to ask her parents for money. She would pawn it more than once.

With no real training, Frances at twenty-seven embarked on a most difficult and dangerous job. She was assigned to find out the facts, and once found, figure out how to prevent the abuses somehow. She was armed only with a pencil and pad when she went out to do investigations of employment offices, train stations, boarding houses, the offices of political "gangs," and police stations. She called them her "haunts."

It was an interesting time in American cities. Manufacturing was booming, including the new industry of automobile production. There were roads to be built! Multitudes of people were tempted into migrating to the cities, with their lure of high-paying jobs. Work-seekers came from the country, the south, and from Europe, all of them in hopes of a better life.

But in Pittsburgh's big steel mills, the city's biggest industry, men worked a twelve-hour day, and many labored seven days a week, too exhausted to take any part in home or community life. Some worked on shifts, not seeing their children for days at a time. The fatigue caused illnesses. The work was dangerous, and led to not only accidents, but deaths. There was no union to put pressure on employers. The steel companies made it their policy to discourage any organizing or improvement. Unskilled male workers averaged less than a dollar and a half a day.

Women had an even harder time. They came to the cities believing they could find respectable work; but in reality, they were often forced into becoming servants, mill workers, or worse, prostitutes, in order to survive.

Diving In Without a Life Preserver

Frances's first job meant fighting on many fronts. She had never been taught how to take a survey, launch new programs, or persuade a city government to take action. It was "on the job training" in the extreme! Uncovering the abuses was not hard, but then she had to come up with the ways to address them. One avenue was to pressure or persuade local officials to pass regulations or laws.

She was asked to give speeches to inform the public of conditions, and to raise money to help effect change. Soon she discovered that she had a talent for public speaking. There were as yet no microphones, but she knew she had a good, strong voice. That may have been thanks to Grandma Perkins, for all those lessons in projecting her voice when she was a child! With each speech she gained more confidence.

As with many endeavors, it was a case of "the more you know, the more you realize you *don't* know!" She wrote, "I knew so little about the whole field of social work." Actually, almost no one did. It was a field in its infancy, as was the whole idea of social workers.

Always thirsty for more knowledge, understanding, and guidance, a contact she approached for information recommended she take some graduate classes. "Do you think they'll let me?" Frances asked. Soon she was enrolled in Saturday and night courses in economics and sociology at the Wharton School of Finance and Commerce, part of the University of Pennsylvania, right in Philadelphia. Fortunately, they had just recently begun to admit women. She later said, "I just lapped it up there. I discovered that I had a mind that... inquires, penetrates, goes to the bottom of things, puts two and two together and comes to some logical conclusions that have authority." But lest you think she was becoming stuffy or full of herself, she wrote to her classmates, "I've also acquired a sense of humor — so that I no longer take myself and my doings so seriously."

Assignment: Danger

Frances discovered that in Philadelphia, rings of unscrupulous men were running a profitable scam. They would meet young women at the train station or wharf, and offer them transportation to a clean, recommended boarding house. Then they would charge an enormous fee for the short ride, amounting to sometimes almost all the money a girl had. Worse yet, the "nice lodging" was usually a brothel, or owned by a manufacturer ready to exploit them. He would staff his factory with desperate women who could be paid slave wages. Or, to make the enterprise look legitimate, sometimes the boarding house would be adequate, but swindlers would arrive to steer girls to an agency that charged huge sums to find them work with employers who were part of the conspiracy. Now the girls were trapped.

First Frances set up a system of volunteers who agreed to regularly meet the new arrivals coming in by boat or train. There needed to be a way to help unsuspecting newcomers avoid these terrible traps.

Of course, she was interrupting a profitable income stream for the criminal-minded men who preyed on young women. They became particularly irate when she helped put a number of the worst and most crooked boarding houses out of business. This made her work dangerous. Decades later, in her *Reminiscences*, she said "I look at it now and realize that it was a very risky and bold thing for me to be in — a young girl who knew nothing. But innocence protects you."

One rainy night, as she walked home alone around eleven o'clock, she realized that she was being followed! Glancing back, she found that two men were in pursuit. She recognized one of them: he was a pimp who ran a corrupt employment agency. She sped up her steps; they walked faster too. "What shall I do?" she thought. Instead of panicking, she recalled what her father had advised her to do in a tough situation. She quickly rounded a corner, stopped short, thrust at them with her umbrella and began to scream, as loudly as she could, the name of the one she knew: "Sam Smith! Sam Smith!" When windows all along the street flew up and heads appeared, the men turned and ran. "What else would you do?"

Frances asked. "It was very funny." Of course, in fact the incident was more frightening than funny.

The close call was the first of many times Frances would use her quick wits in a threatening situation. Imagine the courage that took. Happily, some good came of the heart-pounding incident. She promptly reported it not only to the police and her association, but the people in her organization and some friends who had status in the community.

The next day she went to see two men, the Commissioner of Public Safety and the head of the Bureau of Licenses. One of them told her, "You know we… are just the same. We're Republicans. Over there (at the settlements houses) they're Democrats. But we get together. We fix things up. We handle things for them. They handle things for us. Don't you ever worry, dear Miss Perkins, we'll take care of everything." She called their meeting "a wonderful experience."

As a result, following Frances's interview, city hall closed down not only Smith's corrupt agency, but several others of the worst kind. It also decreed that all lodgings had to now be licensed. The association Frances worked for got to write the licensing rules.

It was a victory, but surely not one she would tell her parents about! She knew her family was "entirely innocent of what went on in social work." She felt it wiser to tell them about the prominent people she occasionally got to meet, leaving out most details of her work. They would not have approved. In fact, they would have been worried sick.

A New Door Opens

One of Frances's professors at the University of Pennsylvania graduate school approached her after one class. He smiled and said, "Miss Perkins, I believe you to be an exceptional student. I enjoy having you here in my class, as you make discussions both deeper and livelier. But you really belong in a top-notch master's degree program. And, you know, there are grants and fellowships available for promising students like you."

With his help, in no time she was accepted to the graduate school of Columbia University in New York and won a $500 fellowship from a foundation. The foundation assigned her a project, a survey of undernourished children in New York City's West Side, an area with the ominous name "Hell's Kitchen."

Another door was opening for Frances, and with it a whole new series of adventures in her third, and largest city, the one we today casually call "The Big Apple."

Chapter 8
New York, New Challenges

Right from the start Frances was in love with New York City. There was no end of exciting places to go and things to do. This was a social and artistic environment that far exceeded what she had known in Chicago and Philadelphia. There were art museums and exhibits to explore, parks to sketch or paint in on sunny Sundays, and quaint little shops and restaurants in Greenwich Village, downtown, arguably the most artsy and picturesque part of Manhattan. She chose to live there because the rents were lower than in uptown neighborhoods. But it was a bonus that it was the neighborhood of artists, musicians, and poets.

It seems her enthusiasm and energy made her shine, and attracted friends. The once shy girl was now always quick to accept an invitation to a bonfire, picnic, ferry ride, or a day on the beaches of Staten Island. She quickly made a great many acquaintances, including some ultimately famous ones: successful authors Theodore Dreiser, who was a magazine editor she met when he rejected a love story she had written under an assumed name, and novelist Sinclair Lewis, who became a close friend and her regular escort.

There were also the popular tea dances to attend. At one she attended in 1910 she spotted a tall, athletic-looking and rather handsome young man. He drew her attention while loudly arguing with someone in defense of his distant cousin, Theodore Roosevelt. Frances asked the friend she'd come with, "And who is *that?*"

"On, that's Franklin Roosevelt. He's an up-and-coming lawyer... and where he *comes* from is money: Harvard, and Columbia. He dabbles in politics too... and goes on pretty wild fishing trips with his buddies, I hear. Let me introduce you."

He looked just as wealthy and privileged as he was. Her first impression was not positive; she felt him a bit arrogant, perhaps too proud and sure of himself.

A Master's Degree from Columbia

Her fellowship assignment was not without its perils. Hell's Kitchen was one of New York's roughest and poorest areas, a district as tough as its name. It wasn't long before she met Thomas MacManus, a senator and political boss of the precinct, so powerful he was known as "*The* MacManus." Some described him as an old-style Irish ward boss. She was aware that most reformers considered him crooked. Ward bosses tended to be!

He was a part of Tammany Hall, a group of city political leaders with a reputation for both powerful influence and corruption. MacManus also chaired the committee on labor and industry in Albany and was the boss of Hell's Kitchen. Tammany held sway over much of New York City and what happened in it. Frances had been warned about MacManus, and his almost unlimited power.

And that is precisely why she marched into his office one day! It must have required backbone to walk through the door. She needed his help, not for herself, but for a teenaged boy who had been arrested for some minor crime and jailed in a place ominously named The Tombs. She learned that the boy's job was the sole means of support for his sisters and mother. While he awaited trial, his family began to starve. When Frances was sent to appeal to a charity organization on behalf of the family, she was turned down, apparently because they believed that one of the children was illegitimate! Frances, however, was not going to let the situation alone. Again, her convictions overrode her fears. Angered, she marched straight to Tammany Hall.

She described Tammany's headquarters as "very roughneck." Stepping inside the door, she found the air thick with the smell of cigar smoke. It was an all-male atmosphere of tobacco spitting, and big talk from men milling about. Yet she plowed forward. Politely she asked, "May I see Mr. MacManus, please?"

"Sure, lady, sure. He'll be glad to see you," one of the men answered.

Led to his office, she found it as full of talking, smoking men as the outer room. But turning to her with his full attention the notorious man, carefully dressed, with a neatly trimmed beard, said, "Go ahead; what's troubling you?"

"Well," she began, "I know a boy and a whole family in trouble. He's in The Tombs awaiting trial."

"Well, I'm always glad to help anybody in trouble. Does he live in this district?"

"Yes."

"What's this boy's name?" Frances recounted the full story of the family's plight. MacManus didn't take much time thinking it over. "Well," he said, "I'll see what I can do. I think I can fix it up. You come around tomorrow."

She did, and he had fixed it up all right. The boy was getting out the very next morning. Frances learned that she didn't necessarily have to like someone, or thoroughly approve of him, to make him an ally.

In June of 1910 she had completed her coursework uptown at Columbia University, submitted her essay, "A Study of Malnutrition in 107 Children from Public School 51," and been awarded her master's degree in political science. (Her coursework, however, was almost completely in economics and sociology.) At Columbia, unlike at Worcester Classical and Mount Holyoke, she had earned many A's.

In her master's essay, she wrote that the statistics on malnutrition were "a mass of documents full of human misery." She concluded that relief (what today we would call welfare) was a stop-gap measure. What was needed, she firmly maintained, was better education and incomes for all. The essay became her first published article in her field.

A New Position

Thanks to the reputation she had built through her work in Philadelphia and New York, that same season she was offered the position of Secretary, or head, of the New York City Consumers' League. She was thrilled that she would now be working for the woman whose enflamed speech at Mount Holyoke had set Frances on her life's path: Florence Kelley, who headed the organization nationwide. This put Frances near the epi-center of the movement for social justice in America.

She was offered a first-year salary of $1,000. It was roughly half what a skilled worker in a trade would make if he had a union behind him. She countered by requesting $1,200 and a full-time stenographer, an assistant who could take dictation in shorthand and transcribe it. She got half of what she asked for, the stenographer, and accepted. She was just 30 years old... and considered herself a "late bloomer."

In her first year with the League Frances worked extensively on three major local problems: sanitary conditions in bakeries; fire prevention in factories; and a bill which if passed would prohibit boys under eighteen and women of any age from working more than fifty-four hours a week.

Ever the ball of energy and drive, she simultaneously took more courses at Columbia and taught a sociology course at Adelphi College on Long Island. As if that wasn't enough, she threw herself into the Votes For Women movement, becoming a skilled soapbox orator!

Most bakeries, especially in poorer areas of the city, were in cellars, with dirty floors, and lacked decent lighting or ventilation. Many had rats and mice, so the bakeries kept cats, which would often jump up on the breadboards, and occasionally deposit a litter of kittens on them! The heat in the summer would cause the sweat to pour off workers into the dough. Toilets or even wash basins were often absent. In some of the filthy basement bakeries, people slept on the floor after working seventeen or eighteen hours.

Frances Goes to Court

When months later Frances was called to testify as an expert on cellar bakeries at the commission's first public hearing, she was not warmly received. "This little girl an expert?!" exclaimed a lawyer hired to defend the real estate interests of the bakeries and their owners. He barraged her with a series of belittling and irrelevant questions concerning whether she had degrees or licenses in medicine or engineering. Of course she had to answer "no, sir" to each. He angrily demanded, "Then by what right do you propose to testify here?" New York State Commissioner and Assemblyman Al Smith responded, "Because we've asked her to."

The lawyer expected Frances to be a pushover, and make an emotional appeal. Instead, she proved to be a worthy foe, armed with hundreds of facts and figures supplied by safety engineers.

Her interrogator was not easily stopped. He loudly proclaimed Frances's lack of training to qualify her as a witness on bakeries, concluding, "She's a totally ignorant and incompetent person and a *girl*, and I protest her being allowed to testify!"

So Smith decided it was his turn to ask witness Frances questions she could answer "yes" to. The last was, "Have you ever been in a cellar bakery?" When she replied again, "Yes, sir," he pronounced with conviction that she was a qualified expert witness. "Give 'em the best you've got," he whispered to Frances. And of course, she did.

After that, bakeries were regulated, and regularly inspected.

Before even finishing her survey of bakeries, she took on another major investigation, that of fire hazards in mills and factories.

She was a whirlwind, always drumming up another investigative report. She had the idea of appealing to teachers to help with yet another priority, pushing for laws to ban child labor. She felt teachers could and *would* help. In speeches at their organizational meetings, she related the statistics: that children were working up to 72-hour weeks in factories where they breathed in fumes and dust. The exposure to such air often led to death. She would end her appeals to an audience of educators with a piece written by a woman, a poem called "Little Toilers."

The golf links lie so near the mills,
That nearly every day,
The laboring children can look out
And see the men at play.

Fighting Fire with Fire

Her no-holds-barred, full-steam-ahead studies of fire safety and prevention were launched when a fire started in a loft in New Jersey. Gasoline had made the third floor of a lamp factory explode. The fire department was located directly across the street. Yet in mere minutes, twenty-five people were dead, with forty more injured. All had been on the fourth floor, but had no means of escape. Nineteen of them had died jumping from the windows. With the huge number of factories in the greater New York City area, the Manhattan Fire Chief predicted that it was just a matter of time before a tragedy of epic proportions struck in the city. He warned that a daytime fire would mean "a terrible loss of life." Frances knew it too. Unfortunately, they were right.

She doubled down on her research into fire problems in industry, especially the lack of adequate exits, fire stairs, sprinkler systems, and other safety devices. She was a "hands-on" kind of investigator, climbing rickety fire escapes, measuring corridor widths, and getting on hands and knees to crawl through narrow escape routes. The last must have been extremely difficult in long skirts; women as yet never wore pants.

Chapter 9

Fire Enflames Frances

On the 25th of March, a warm spring Saturday afternoon in 1911, Frances was enjoying some down time by having tea with friends at a neighbor's lovely house in Greenwich Village. She'd been hard at work on getting the legislature in Albany to pass a bill limiting the weekly working hours of women and boys to fifty-four hours. She'd just entertained her girlfriends with a tale about her dealings with a difficult but colorful character, the influential Tammany Hall political boss known as "Big Tim" Sullivan, complete with an imitation of his Irish accent, when they heard fire engines clanging. The circle of friends immediately put down their teacups and ran across the park, Washington Square, to see what was on fire. Flames were leaping from the upper floors, the lofts, of a ten-story wooden factory building. Now a sweatshop operation, it had been designed for storage only. Inside were roughly 600 employees finishing up their work day at the Triangle Shirtwaist Company, which made women's blouses. With scraps of fabric everywhere, the building went up like a match thrown into a haystack.

Frances and her friends stood in the street looking up with horror. On the tenth floor a few people managed to climb to the roof and leap to safety in the adjacent building. But most workers panicked. The two elevators quickly broke and the one fire escape, in a light shaft, soon proved to be a death trap. There was one staircase, which soon filled with suffocating smoke. Many workers died piled up at the bottom of it, where they found a locked door. *Why?* Employers had locked the doors to prevent any risk of stealing, and to keep union organizers out.

The fire fighters had ladders, but they weren't tall enough to reach the eighth floor where the fire had broken out. Nets were tried, but from such a height, the leaping women crashed right through them. Workers crowded to the windows while firemen yelled to them not to jump. What can you do in the panic of a life and death situation when it is far too high for you to jump to safety? When there are flames roaring at your back, you jump anyway. Frances saw one young woman hang from a window sill until the flames scorched her hands. Others jumped only after their clothes caught fire. A few covered their eyes with pieces of cloth so as to not see their friends, dead on the pavement below. Not one person survived the fall. Scores of others were burned to death in the loft of the building, trampled underfoot, or crushed to death by the mad fight for the elevators.

Frances stood on the sidewalk below and saw it all, a scene out of hell. She wrote many years later that the scene "struck at the pit of my stomach." But she did not cover her eyes or turn away.

In only about a half hour, 146 lost their lives. All but fifteen were young women, many of them recent Italian and Jewish arrivals. Fully half of all the dead were teenagers, as young as fourteen. Most of the rest were in their twenties. Another seventy-one were injured, scarred for life, physically and emotionally.

The Back Story

The fire in the wooden building had become an inferno in just minutes due to the conditions inside. Oiled sewing machines were packed close together, with highly flammable pattern pieces and scraps of cloth piled on the floors and in overflowing baskets.

The district fire chief was interviewed by the *New York Tribune* newspaper. He declared, "This calamity is just what I have been predicting. There were no outside fire escapes on this building. The large loss of life is due to this neglect."

Incredibly, the workers at this factory had gone out on strike only a year earlier. They were among the first female strikers in American labor history. Among their top demands were unlocked doors and working fire escapes. But the owners would not talk with the strikers, even though they had formed a small union to present a united front. Instead, the company hired temporary replacement workers known as "scabs" to cross the picket lines. Then they fired every worker who had joined the union. Eventually the remaining workers had no choice but to starve or return to their labors behind the locked doors of Triangle.

A Firestorm of Reaction

The public rose up to demand that laws be passed to make conditions such as these illegal. The tragedy galvanized Frances and filled her with angry resolve. She became determined that people be shocked into action. More inspiration came in the aftermath of the fire. The people of New York were angry too. More than 3,500 poured into the Metropolitan Opera House for a mass memorial meeting eight days after the disaster. Many important men spoke, including city officials, social workers, and clergymen. They all pushed for reforms, and donations for the survivors and the families of the dead. But for Frances, the one truly riveting speaker was a petite young woman with fiery red hair. Her name was Rose Schneiderman. She was the head of the Women's Trade Union League. She had a fiery tongue as well.

Rose's speech began softly but gradually built to a dramatic crescendo. She said the lives of workers were being held cheap while property was considered sacred. She cried, "Every year thousands of us are maimed... every week I must learn of the untimely death of one of my sister workers!" The passions of all in the crowd were stirred. Schneiderman was destined to become a lifelong friend of Perkins.

Frances, electrified, found she was not alone. What followed was a tsunami of public outrage. From a gathering of a few thousand grew a march estimated at 120,000 for the long funeral procession of six unidentified victims. Over 400,000 people lined the streets to watch the silent march. No music was played; there was just grim silence and the sound of footsteps as the throngs passed by.

The unidentified bodies were buried in coffins at a cemetery bordering two New York boroughs, Brooklyn and Queens. The mass grave has a tall monument with an image of a kneeling, grieving woman.

In fact, the Triangle Shirtwaist Company had met all the fire requirements that existed when the building was finished in 1901. Even though they had had eight fires in nine years, the managers refused to hold fire drills. Eventually a trial by jury followed. Appallingly, the factory owners not only went free, but collected handsomely from their insurance company for their lost property. The building owner settled a couple of dozen individual law suits by families of people who had died. He paid out just $75 per life. Imagine.

As for Frances, she became convinced that the Triangle disaster could be the catalyst for major reform in the United States. Decades later she would state, "The New Deal was born on March 25th, 1911." It had taken a tragedy of major proportions, but progress began soon after, with the formation of two major "blue ribbon" committees. They were a Factory Investigating Commission set up by the state legislature, and the Committee on Safety of the City of New York.

Our budding superhero was an advisor to both, and an expert witness when repeatedly called upon. No wonder: she had in the previous year made fire safety her top priority and learned everything she could by interviewing fire fighters, building designers, engineers, and specialists in fire prevention. The members of the Committee on Safety knew they needed a strong leader to command attention and get things done. Frances was rapidly appointed Executive Director. She may have been unaware of it at the time, but the suggestion that she be appointed head had come down from on high: from none other than one of her early idols, former President Theodore Roosevelt.

Frances The Lobbyist

Increasingly she took the train to Albany, the state capital, to lobby congressmen and senators on legislation. She committed herself to fight on a number of fronts. Factory reform was a priority, but so were working hours. The bill to limit working hours for boys and women faced much opposition. This bill meant a great deal to her. She knew well the suffering caused when women and children were required to work insufferable hours. For over a year she made weekly trips to push for the bill's passage. She button-holed and befriended Senator Al Smith, the future governor.

She got prominent members of the Consumers' League's board to host parties at which legislators had the importance of the reform impressed upon them. In the end, Smith, who was to become another life-long friend and ally, helped persuade others to back the bill.

She found another major ally in an influential state Senator, "Big Tim" Sullivan, earlier known in NYC as "the King of the Bowery," a lower Manhattan district. After much lobbying, Sullivan was won over. He agreed to cast his vote for the bill, and did, then left to catch a boat for New York City. Suddenly she had a crisis on her hands! In Sullivan's absence, opponents to the bill had managed to sway enough legislators to change their vote to defeat it.

Did Frances take it lying down? Did she say to herself, "Oh well, maybe next year we'll win?" No! She leapt into action. She convinced a supporter to call for the bill to be reconsidered, then raced to a phone to call the captain and beg him to hold the boat at the dock. Big Tim Sullivan, good to his pledge of support, rushed back in a taxi. When it stalled along the route, he ran the rest of the way, arriving just in time before the doors were locked for the night. As he came in, he gasped to Frances in his Irish American dialect, "It's all right, me girl, we is with you." He persuaded just enough senators to change their votes. After five years of effort, the fifty-four-hour bill was finally passed.

Senator Smith told Frances, "You pulled a smart one. That was very smart. I didn't think you had the courage to do it." Frances was never short on courage. She was willing to make sacrifices. She had planned a summer vacation to Europe with friends, and got teased by Smith about her decision to stay home if there might be even a slight chance of the vote being taken. It was lucky she did.

The Safety Committee

As leader of the Committee on Safety, an inspired idea she had was to take the commission members on factory tours around New York. Maybe she recalled what a wake-up call her field trips in college had been. Let's hear her tell about how she took the future governor and others for a series of surprise outings, the equivalent of pop quizzes, to see the women, thousands of them, coming off the ten-hour night shift on rope walks.

We made sure that Robert Wagner (the committee's chairman, and a future U.S. Senator) personally crawled through the tiny hole in the wall that gave egress to a steep iron ladder covered with ice and ending twelve feet from the ground which was euphemistically labeled "Fire Escape" in many factories. We saw to it that the austere legislative members of the Commission got up at dawn and drove with us for an unannounced visit to a cannery and that they saw with their own eyes the little children, not adolescents, but five, six, and seven-

year-olds, snipping beans and shelling peas. We made sure that they saw the machinery that would scalp a girl or cut off a man's arm. Hours so long that both men and women were depleted and exhausted became realities to them through seeing for themselves their dirty little factories.

On one occasion a member of the committee, a Republican from Rochester, declared there *were no* children working in the State of New York.

So, we took them out one fine morning, getting them all to rise at four o'clock, and popped them into a factory that was just full of children at that hour in the morning - a surprise visit. We took them to several other places. They saw children at work. You never could tell (them) again that children didn't work in the State of New York.

These experiences had such a powerful effect that after the commission wrote its final report, things started to change. New York State was rapidly becoming the national leader in improving working conditions, including sanitation, ventilation, and all sorts of safety measures.

In all, thirty-three laws were passed, including one that for the first time provided payments, called compensation, to workers injured on the job. In her memoirs she said the legislation passed in New York "marked a change in American political attitudes and policies toward social responsibility... It was, I am convinced, a turning point."

The irony of course was that Frances herself could not yet vote, being female.

Perk Changes Her Image

It began with a small incident in the state house while she toiled as a lobbyist. A certain senator was charged with heading up a commission to investigate the governor, a task he found emotionally upsetting. One day Frances, who was not well acquainted with the senator, had him approach her and a strange thing happened: "He grabbed me by the hand, he wrung it," and he began an emotional appeal to her, sobbing, "Oh, Miss Perkins, we've done a terrible thing!" His committee had just voted to impeach the governor, and the senator, a member of the same party, felt like a traitor, going on, "I tried to save him myself... It's so dreadful!" After wiping his tears away with his handkerchief he added, "Every man's got a mother, you know."

At first the startled young lobbyist thought of the encounter as a funny little story, and passed it on to a friend. But then she began to analyze what was behind it. She summed up her conclusions thus: "I learned from this that the way men take women in political life is to associate them with motherhood. They know and respect their mothers… I said to myself 'that's the way to get things done.'" She decided to adopt a totally different look than she had as a fashionable young woman in New York City: "to behave, dress and act to remind them subconsciously of their mothers. It was not long afterwards that I adopted the black dress with the bow of white at the throat as kind of an official uniform. It has always worked," she declared years later.

At the time of this permanent alteration she was all of thirty-three years old.

The downside of the new look she affected, topped off by her trademark tricorn, was the press, which had sometimes in the past referred to her as "perky" or "pretty," now called her "Mother Perkins" or worse yet, "Ma Perkins,"(a funny character in a radio show), labels she detested.

Frances, Feminist

Instead of stewing about the injustice of being treated as a second-class citizen, unable to vote, she renewed her efforts to right this major wrong, standing on street corners atop a wooden fruit crate or soap box under a "Women's Suffrage" banner. Being Frances, she quickly learned to turn hecklers and snide or angry comments to her advantage using wit and funny little stories. She reasoned, "If the crowd laughs with you once, they're for you, and not the fellow who's bothering you."

Not until 1920, when the Nineteenth Amendment to the Constitution was passed, were all American women granted the right to vote. The fight for suffrage had been waged since the 1860's, with women in growing numbers marching, petitioning, and protesting. Men said women did not have the intellectual capacity or sense to be voters. Opponents said suffrage would destroy the family. One U.S.

senator said having the vote would lead to "government by females" and recommended that women "attach themselves to some man who will represent them in public affairs." Another predicted "disaster and ruin would overtake the nation" if women voted.

Susan B. Anthony, the mother of the women's rights movement, actually did manage to vote in 1872. She was promptly arrested, jailed, and found guilty of the crime.

After years of struggle, the fight for votes for women intensified. Suffragists were everywhere. Newspapermen usually called them "suffragettes," the diminutive, feminine version of the word, to minimize and mock their efforts, first in England, and then in the U.S. Those who picketed the White House and other government sites were arrested and imprisoned. If they courageously protested their treatment by going on hunger strikes, they suffered forced feeding, via tubes inserted into their nostrils or forced down their throats.

Her closest women friends in New York were also suffragists. They often went out in pairs for moral support when speaking on the street, garnering support and winning over foes with gentle humor. She remembered years later, "Women learned to like each other in that suffrage movement… they played fair and supported each other. These were the people who would stand by me when I was in trouble."

At one feminist gathering, Frances used her turn at the podium to tell the crowd that dramatic change was needed in the relations between men and women in society, and that "feminism means revolution." She wrote to her quite conservative Mount Holyoke classmates that her work on the campaign for suffrage was serious.

In 1915, wearing the suffragists' colors of gold, purple, and white, she was part of the Great Suffrage Parade in New York, where twenty-five thousand women and men marched all the way from Greenwich Village downtown, up Fifth Avenue to 59th Street, while huge crowds of spectators cheered and marching bands played.

But the struggle was not to be over for another decade. Although in New York women won voting rights in 1918, not until the Nineteenth Amendment to the

Constitution was passed in 1920 could American women everywhere cast their vote and be represented by their government.

More Firsts

We've already seen Frances Perkins' dedication to social justice and her defense of workers and their families result in amazing progress for a young woman in the first dozen years of the new century. Remember that at the time, extremely few women were employed in fields other than teaching, nursing, and domestic work. Even those were nearly all unmarried, as wives were still almost universally expected by society to remain in the home. That is, unless you were poor. Society's dictates did not apply to women who were not middle or upper class, and therefore "respectable."

Frances's "famous firsts" for women were never accidental or due to luck. Her ferocious work ethic and dedication to the causes she saw as critical drove her onward. The world was finding her work could not be ignored, because she had made herself an expert in many areas.

Her respect for higher education matched her work ethic. Back in Philadelphia, she had studied economics and sociology, even while doing social work for the Philadelphia Research and Protective Association. This dual commitment opened more doors for her.

Her persistence in lobbying for change in Albany continued to draw the admiration of Al Smith, the state senator who had been her ally in court and was greatly impressed when she fought for the fifty-four-hour bill and other legislation. This friendship was to help pave the way to future success. One accomplishment led to another as Frances's achievements brought her growing respect and renown. During the 1920's she even found time to head the Council on Immigrant Education.

Her star was rising. Bigger things were yet to come.

Chapter 10

Frances Finds Love

Frances was enjoying a rich, personal life apart from her work. One of the benefits of living in New York was mixing and mingling in a large social circle, which even included some prominent writers. One of them, author Sinclair Lewis, became her frequent date. He apparently fell in love with her, and one warm night when all the windows were open, proposed to her from the street loudly enough for the neighbors to hear. It seemed he'd had a drink or two. Neither one took the proposal seriously. Years later he based the central character in one of his novels chiefly on Frances.

When she reached age thirty, Frances's parents had resigned themselves to their daughter remaining single. But then she met Paul Wilson, who was moving in the same social circles. Four years older, he was an intelligent and highly educated man and attractive, with thick, dark, wavy hair. Paul was also athletic, particularly on the tennis court. And he dressed impeccably.

On a variety of outings with mutual friends, their relationship slowly progressed. They had not only lots of friends in common, but many mutual interests. In 1905 he had left a career in business to join the movement to reform politics. He worked at first for a non-profit organization dedicated to exposing government corruption and misuse of money. He and Frances had shared values. And they were attracted to one another.

Still, Frances, who had not planned on making room for marriage in her life, was not easily won over to the idea. She wrote many years later, "Young girls marry at eighteen or twenty-two… having passed that period without fatal commitments, I was on the whole rather anxious *not* to marry."

So Paul had to be persistent. And patient! Their letters to one another whenever apart over three years show the gradual progression. Toward the end of 1910 he signed letters to Frances, "Yours with Sincere Regards." But the next year he wrote,

"I wish I could visit all the places dear to you... God bless you, dear Frances." By 1913, it was clear that both were madly in love. Before their wedding, while she was vacationing at the family home in Newcastle, Maine, she wrote every day, and sometimes even twice a day, sending some letters by special delivery. In a letter of eight pages describing her loneliness without him, she wrote "To think I write you like this!! I am a different woman. I am indeed."

Paul responded, "You and your perfect love have the power to make me see things anew. I adore and worship you, beloved, dearly beloved."

It was as private a wedding as is possible. They were married in the little chapel of Grace Episcopal church in downtown New York without a word to anyone except, at the last minute, their parents, whom they did not invite to attend. The two people who signed the marriage certificate as witnesses were strangers coaxed from the street and pressed into service. The newlyweds sent a simple white card to all their friends and relatives: "Paul C. Wilson and Francis Perkins announce their marriage, September 26th, 1913."

Florence Kelly offered the couple her cliffside Maine cottage with a view of the sea for a brief honeymoon. They had hoped to take a honeymoon trip of several months to Europe the next summer following the mayoral election Paul was involved in. It was not to be. Archduke Ferdinand of Austria was assassinated. Europe and then America were quickly entangled in events that thrust them toward the First World War, also called "The Great War," and then "The War to End All Wars."

Miss Perkins or Mrs. Wilson?

Frances and her husband discussed whether she would change her name upon marriage. A woman keeping her maiden name is fairly common today, but was almost unheard of in 1913. Not to become Frances Wilson went completely against tradition. But her work had given her name considerable authority and recognition which would be lost if she became Mrs. Paul Wilson. Moreover, there was still a strong prejudice against married women working at all. But the primary reason she chose to remain Frances Perkins was to avoid a conflict of interest, or the appearance of one. Paul was employed as an assistant to the mayor of New

York City. How could she speak out against, say, the city's fire prevention policy, without jeopardizing her husband's position if she were Mrs. Paul Wilson? Years later she said that she had also acted on feminist principles: "My generation was perhaps the first that openly and actively asserted — at least some of us did — the separateness of women and their personal independence in the family relationship."

It was not a decision that many were ready to accept. Before the couple had been married two weeks, a reporter and photographer were at the door demanding an explanation. Even Mount Holyoke insisted on addressing mail to her as Mrs. Paul C. Wilson. More than once she corrected them, writing "I do not use husband's name socially or professionally or legally." Her own insurance company, on a life insurance policy she took out, wanted to call her "Frances Perkins Wilson, alias Frances Perkins." She had to pay an attorney to prove that a married woman was *not* legally required to change her name, but that it was a mere custom.

She won the day with the insurance company, but in her future role as a public servant, critics always made her name an issue to use against her, or, as one biographer put it, "a club to beat her with."

Woodrow Wilson became president in the year Frances and Paul were married, and in order to help workers, the president proposed a new cabinet office: the United States Department of Labor. It was quickly approved by Congress.

Paul was busy working as the economic advisor to the mayor of New York. Frances continued long hours of work with the Committee on Safety and the Factory Investigation Commission, as well as working on unemployment problems. But she secretly dreamed of cutting back on her career and making room for a new addition.

Starting a Family

It was not to be easy. Not until 1915 was she expecting a baby. But sadly her first pregnancy ended in a miscarriage. Before long she was expecting again. This time there were serious health complications. Frances developed a very dangerous pregnancy- related condition that caused sudden spikes in blood pressure. She continued work, but mostly from her bed. Her doctors had told her that both her life and her baby's life were at risk. A letter to Paul showed her dread of the worst. Before going to the hospital, she wrote instructions for him on naming and nurturing their baby should she die. At the maternity ward, she delivered a boy by caesarean section. But the baby was either stillborn or died within a day or two. Paul and Frances, grief-stricken, were never able to talk about their lost baby to friends. Frances's full recovery was slow.

But badly wanting a child, they tried a third time and toward the end of 1916 Frances finally gave birth to a perfect baby girl they named Susanna Perkins Wilson. Her parents were ecstatic. Susanna enjoyed her first summer sojourn to the Maine homestead as a nine-month-old, delighting in crawling on the lawn. Paul remained behind in New York working, but wrote regularly, missing them. One letter closed with, "In my arms, in my eyes, seeing I cannot do anything so well without you.... I adore you, I admire you and rely upon you greatly. Your lover, Paul."

Frances however was never without a new project or a cause close to her heart. Having had a serious brush with death and lost an infant, she threw herself into the challenge of heading up a new group: The Maternity Center Association. She had learned that New York was one of the most hazardous cities in which to have a baby, especially if you were poor, malnourished, or an immigrant. After convincing wealthy donors to help the Women's City Club of New York fund the project, Frances hired a small army of nurses. They made thousands of home visits to pregnant women and new mothers, providing free care for over 1,600 patients in their first year. They constantly expanded the number of clinics they operated. As the program grew, lives were saved: deaths of mothers dropped by 60 percent, and 29 percent more babies survived. The association became a training ground for nurses and doctors coming from all over the world to learn the latest methods. Frances stayed on the board of the organization for more than two decades. The Association, still in existence, might never have thrived if Frances had not been its first Executive Secretary. Her position was unsalaried. Not until after women had the vote did Congress finally pass a bill extending health services for mothers and children throughout the United States.

Clouds on the Home Front

All was not as Frances had hoped for at home. Her husband took it very hard when the mayor he worked for was crushed in the next election. He grew despondent. He didn't even follow up on a valuable lead for a new position. Paul deteriorated more and more. It became clear that he was suffering from psychological problems. Rarely would Frances discuss his condition with anyone, but at one point told a friend, "It was always up and down. He was sometimes depressed, sometimes excited." She called it "an up-and-down illness."

What she was describing was at the time a mysterious condition later called Manic Depression. Today we call it Bipolar Disorder. Often hereditary, its main symptoms are extreme emotional highs and lows. Although there is no cure, today we have better medicines and therapies to help people who are bipolar.

The situation grew very difficult for Frances, as it became increasingly obvious that Paul could not work or take on any responsibility. Frances sent her husband for the best care available at sanitariums and in hospitals, all of it costly. The family resources had been exhausted when Paul unwisely speculated with the money he'd inherited, losing it all. Financial recklessness can be another symptom of the disease. With no other relatives or resources to rely on, Frances realized it was all up to her to provide for the family. Later on, she confessed that she "had to hustle to see us through that crisis." She knew that she could not count on Paul recovering, and must prepare for their future.

Meanwhile, America, which had at first stayed out of World War I, joined the fight. President Wilson and Congress declared war on Germany in April of 1917. There was a great nationwide scramble to get ready. Frances did her part by volunteering to head up relief efforts in New York City.

At the same time, she plunged into another volunteer effort: the campaign to elect Al Smith to be Governor of New York. She had known him since her early days lobbying in Albany and knew him to be committed to labor reform. She threw herself wholeheartedly into the fight, realizing it would not be easy: New York had never before elected a governor who was not a Protestant. Smith was a Roman Catholic.

Fannie at 3
Courtesy of the Frances Perkins Center

Fannie as a teenager
Courtesy Tomlin Perkins Coggeshall

"The Brick House"
at the Perkins Family
Homestead, circa 1900

Courtesy
Tomlin Perkins Coggeshall

Frederick Perkins
Frances Perkins papers
Columbia University

Fannie as a Junior at Mount Holyoke
Mount Holyoke College Archives

Leading her Mount Holyoke graduation
procession as Class President

Mount Holyoke College Archives

Frances inspecting a New York City
fire escape ladder, 1911

Courtesy of Columbia University

FIRE: The Shirtwaist Factory ablaze

Pen and Ink by Ruth Monsell

Long line to identify victims of
the Shirtwaist Factory fire
at the morgue, March 25, 1911
Courtesy of the Library of Congress

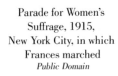

Parade for Women's
Suffrage, 1915,
New York City, in which
Frances marched
Public Domain

Newlyweds Paul Wilson and
Frances Perkins, Newcastle, 1914
Frances Perkins Center

Paul holding Susanna, about 1920
Frances Perkins Center

With two New York businessmen,
after organizing a National Governors
Conference on the Depression
Public Domain

Portrait of Frances, about 1925
Frances Perkins Center

With Susanna, after being appointed
New York State Industrial Commissioner
Albany, New York
UPI, Bettman

Little girl as caregiver to her baby
sister, in between her shifts at
a factory
Library of Congress

Three young cutters at a fish
packing plant. Little fingers
were often cut open by
the sharp knives
Library of Congress

Children working in a
Tennessee garment factory.
Note the flammable fabric
scraps covering the floor
*Courtesy National Archives
and Records Administration*

Two New York Governors,
Franklin Roosevelt and Al Smith.
Smith served four terms as Governor,
followed by FDR, 1929-1932.
Courtesy Columbia University

Unemployed men thronging
outside City Hall, Cleveland
in 1930
Public Domain

Child watching her father cover milk to prevent spoilage in their Hooverville camp
Public Domain

Farm Worker and his family. The Farm Security Administration (FSA),
a New Deal agency, worked to help and house farming families
Public Domain

Chapter 11
The Governor Calls

It was 1919. In a squeaker of an election, Smith had won. Weeks after his inauguration a factory inspector she knew came into her office.

"I want to be the first to congratulate you," he crowed.

"For what?" a puzzled Frances asked.

"Why, you're going to be a member of the New York State Industrial Commission," he told her.

Frances laughed heartily at what she was sure was a crazy notion. She was certain no governor would appoint a woman to oversee conditions in factories, a coveted job with a big salary. When a few weeks passed with nothing more said, she forgot about it, busy with her two-year-old and unhealthy spouse. When Smith finally called Perkins to the state capital in Albany, she was sure he wanted to talk about changes to the child labor law. She was wrong.

"We'll talk about that later," said the governor. "I was thinkin'. How'd you like to be a member of the Industrial Commission in Albany?" It was a group whose work was close to her heart, as it set safety standards in factories, supervised people who inspected them, and made decisions on compensation for workers injured on the job.

The usually outspoken Frances was tongue-tied. Speechless. The notion was so startling! No woman had ever before been appointed to an administrative post in New York. She blurted out, "How did you get the idea of appointing me... it's so unusual!" Smith had several reasons. He knew his commission was in terrible shape and wanted someone strong and experienced to shape it up. He believed that now that women were about to have the vote, he "ought to bring women into the political picture," and had known Frances a long time in Albany and beyond.

He told her, "I remembered that when you were appearing before committees, you had somethin' to say. You said it quick, you said it clear, and I could understand it. I knew, too, what you said was true — I could rely on it. When you got through, you sat down. That's more than most people can do."

Instead of accepting on the spot, she said there was one person whose advice she wanted first. It was Florence Kelley. Frances feared that the leader she most looked up to would want her to continue independent social work rather than to be part of a political administration with its compromises and deal making.

Smith threw her a little zinger: "If you girls are going to get what you want through legislation, there better not be any separation between social workers and the government!"

Frances need not have feared Florence Kelley. Frances got back to Manhattan just in time to catch Florence in Pennsylvania Station about to catch a train. It wasn't the ideal setting for a delicate, probing conversation, but over coffee, Frances confided the job offer. The older woman reacted by breaking down in tears, and exclaiming, "Glory be to God! ... I never thought I would live to see the day when someone we had trained, who knew about industrial conditions, cared about women, ...would have the chance to be an administrative officer!"

Frances thought about her grandmother, Cynthia Otis Perkins, who always said, "If someone opens a door for you, unexpectedly... walk right in and do the best you can." She accepted.

Backlash

Of course, there was a firestorm of outrage. Many men were simply in an uproar that the appointment went to a woman. Labor leaders complained that she was not a union member. Others charged she was taking a place that should go to a manufacturer, or at least a businessman. Some envied that she would be highly paid. But Smith stood by her, touted her qualifications, and prevailed. Frances's hometown paper proclaimed in its banner headline, "Fanny Perkins, Former Worcester Girl, Gets $8000 Job and Starts a Rumpus." An original of the front page was displayed, framed, in the front hall of The Brick House.

Though a city businessmen's organization called her "too radical" and *the New York Times* predicted a bitter confirmation fight, she was confirmed by a vote of 34 to 16, with thirteen Republicans supporting her.

This was to be her first government job in an exclusively male environment. It was the world she would spend most of her lifetime negotiating. In the course of it, she would be repeatedly attacked in the press, resented, and threatened. She knew she had to develop a thick skin, and did. Of being a novelty as a woman in government, she said in her seventies,

> *I became a judge in workmen's compensation, a new idea at the time, and I realized that some of the old lawyers and insurance company representatives, as well as the injured men, took it pretty hard. I tried to remind them of their mothers, and it worked. They could take justice at the hands of a woman who reminded them of their mothers. . . Many women dress in ways that are very attractive and pretty, but don't particularly invite confidence in their common sense, integrity or sense of justice.*

This approach was what the times seemed to require, and she felt that her motherly, middle-aged persona helped make her less threatening and more acceptable in a man's world.

Because Frances Perkins accepted the post, New York became a leader in labor legislation and management. Frances saw to it that the department ran efficiently and was productive. Soon other states were modeling theirs after New York's.

For example, under her leadership, the 54-hour work week law was changed to a 47-hour law. And now, women and children were limited to eight-hour work days. (Working on Saturdays was still the norm.)

Meanwhile, Frances was becoming an expert on unemployment, one of her chief interests. She created a system to track and report trends in employment in about 2,000 factories in the state. This helped gauge employment throughout the country. New York statistics and predictions came to be regarded as more reliable than those of the Federal Government's Department of Labor!

Workplace safety was not only about machinery and fire exits. Frances's degree in the sciences was an asset on the job. She found that factory accidents sometimes led to scientific discoveries. For example, unexplained explosions were happening in factories. To investigate, she set up a nationwide study. She appointed experts on safety, fire marshals, factory inspectors, and scientists to study the problem. Together they discovered that dust explodes when mixed with air in some electrical conditions. Immediately Frances created a code to regulate conditions in industries that created dust. She believed that whenever workers were at risk on the job, the country had a moral responsibility to correct and regulate that condition. Many new chemicals were being used in manufacturing for the first time, especially after 1920. Some of them exposed workers to high levels of lead or carbon monoxide. Occupational diseases followed.

Silicosis, a terrible disease of the lungs, was one of them. It occurred when dust became airborne, such as during drilling and grinding. Even polishing pearl buttons on a daily basis without proper ventilation could cause dust and grit to be inhaled. Over time, it could cause suffocation.

Frances thought up the bright idea of running a statewide contest. It offered a reward of several hundred dollars to whoever could discover the best way to prevent workers from inhaling silica dust. After the prize was awarded, she cleverly arranged to have the resulting new device tested. It was installed on the jackhammers excavating the foundation of a new building complex: New York City's famous Rockefeller Center. Because the workers using the jackhammers were tested for silicosis both before and after the project, they knew the new device worked. In this way Frances had proof that workers could be protected. That proof led to new laws requiring protection.

Now that Frances was a duly appointed official with the authority to effect real change, the world had begun to see the stuff she was made of. She went on to become not just a commissioner, but the chair of the Industrial Board, and then the head of the New York State Department of Labor. She also began to attract some very positive press. A British reporter wrote, after seeing her in action, "I have met many interesting women in the United States, but none who has impressed me more... with her shrewd, alert face, keen wide-set eyes, and warmly human personality.... She has won every inch of her way to the high office she now holds by service, efficiency, and a remarkable combination of humor." The quote summed her up well.

On the Front Lines: Her First Strike

It was 1919, and Perkins, newly appointed as a member of the Industrial Commission, found herself in charge of mediation and arbitration overseeing labor disputes and helping to settle strikes between workers and employers. It was the first strike in which she would go to the site of the conflict, and it was a doozy. Upstate in a city called Rome, almost the entire labor force, over four thousand copper workers, walked off their jobs. Many of the workers spoke limited English, as they had immigrated from Italy. Frances knew they had just cause to strike. They'd been assigned longer hours without any pay raise, though they were already earning less than other workers in the northeast doing the same jobs. They also wanted an eight-hour day. Meanwhile, the owners of Rome's five copper manufacturing companies were making fortunes and building mansions. Yet those same owners and employers refused to even meet with the workers and hear their grievances.

When the laborers made attempts to talk with a key employer-owner, a Mr. Spargo, he abused them with foul language, and knocked some down a flight of stairs.

The violence worsened. Some workers attacked Spargo with a knife, and he had to be rescued by others in the crowd. Spargo in retaliation drove a car through a group of striking men and fired a gun into the crowd. Miraculously no one was killed. But the situation was so volatile that Rome's mayor asked Governor Smith to send state police to "quell the riot." Owners still refused to negotiate. The impasse had been going on for a month.

Into this cauldron Frances courageously stepped. Other commissioners in Albany thought it unnecessary, but Frances decided, and Smith agreed, that having a commissioner on site might be helpful. "I felt I had to go," she said. She took a night train to Albany, where another bureau mediator, a Mr. Downey, joined her. On arriving in Rome, there was a lengthy debate as to whether to let them get off; the conductor said he had orders not to let any passengers leave the train, because shots had been fired.

Nevertheless, she persuaded the conductor to relent. Eventually, she and Downey got off the train and into a taxi. But on the bridge into town, they found their way blocked by a large mob of angry workers with guns and rocks. Un-daunted, Downey reminded the workers that he was a mediator, and introduced Frances as an industrial commissioner. She made a little speech, assuring the men that she had come to listen to them, hear their grievances, and talk with their em-ployers. They let her pass.

Frances spent days speaking with all parties and quickly learned the biggest problem: the mayor and the owners' lawyer had convinced the governor to call out the state police. They were already massed just outside Rome, ready to move in. On the other side, the strikers were arming to fight back. And worse yet, an insider, labor organizer John Flynn, told Frances that the strikers had a hidden stockpile of dynamite.

Talk about an explosive situation! Frances agonized over it, but decided she simply had to avoid bloodshed in Rome. Though she didn't tell Governor Smith about the explosives, she managed to persuade him to remove the state police forces from the area. Once she knew they were withdrawing, she boldly marched into the town square, stood on a bench and made another speech. She decided to orchestrate a deal. First, she made a plea for cooperation from everyone, stressing law and order. One of the strike leaders was a man named Ludovicci. Frances knew only a few words of Italian, so after she'd exhausted them, Ludovicci took over. He explained to the gathered crowd that Perkins knew they had dynamite hidden. He added that she had promised the governor that they would get rid of it as soon as the state police were gone.

The bargain worked. Men disappeared, many to basements, and she later re-called, "It was extraordinary… They came up with loads (of dynamite) in suitcases and bags,… I remember one man put it on a baby carriage — one by one, two by two, they went over toward the canal and dumped it in."

There was great relief, but of course the strike still had to be settled. Frances convinced three other commission members to hold an official hearing in Rome about two weeks after she had arrived there. The courthouse was packed. Even the adjacent park and the steps outside were crowded. Workers gave their testimonies first; then lawyers for the employers spoke.

Spargo, who was at the center of the firestorm, had left town, but not before sending an inflammatory letter full of extremely foul and abusive language to the strikers. Naturally its effect was to further infuriate the workers. Frances herself was outraged that almost none of the actual factory owners or employers were available at the hearing. They believed that to appear and speak was a concession to the workers. Their lawyers stated that they would absolutely not recognize any workers' union. Hours of discussion went by, and no progress was made... until Frances decided to play her trump card.

Only two other commissioners knew what that was: the workers had entrusted Spargo's obscene and hate-filled letter to Frances. Finally, she pulled it from her handbag and told her colleague John Mitchell, who was chairing the hearing, that he would have to read it out loud. She knew that it would make clear exactly how and why the workers felt so degraded and enraged.

Mr. Mitchell told the courtroom it was his duty to read Spargo's letter, but that it would be vile and painful. For one thing, in that era, almost no one used such profanities, especially in public and in front of women! First, he spoke movingly of the workers:

They live here. They work here. They must be treated like human beings, and when they are not, the resentments that gather are terrible indeed. Because they have been so insulted, they are insistent on having what they believe to be right and just and having it guaranteed by the State Industrial Commission.

But before Mitchell could actually begin reading the Spargo letter, an employer jumped up to prevent it, stating that no other employer would have written such a letter. When there was applause throughout the audience, he pledged, finally, to reach an agreement with his workers the very next day, if only Mitchell would not read that letter. His brave speech led to all the Rome employers agreeing to match the wages paid to brass and copper workers in Connecticut. The strike was quickly ended.

Frances's courage, cool head and quick thinking, and the card she had kept up her sleeve, had saved the day. Returning to Albany, she regaled Governor Smith with the full story, this time including the dynamite. His response was, "You sure had your nerve with you. It was a risky business all right. But now it's all over and I congratulate you, Commissioner."

Frances had proven she was not only heroic in her words and her actions for social justice, but was brave enough to risk placing herself in the line of fire.

Keep in mind that this was all more than a century ago. Governor Smith had heard it from all directions that he should have his head examined for sending a *woman* to negotiate a major labor strike. But back upstate, one of the top officials of the Rome Brass and Copper Company said to their lawyer, "Do us a favor and ask the governor where he found that woman!"

Frances had immense respect for Governor Smith. It was he who had first taught her about lobbying. They had worked together for nine years and become fast friends and allies by the time Smith won the Democratic nomination for President of the United States in 1928. They shared a commitment to the same goals regarding work hours, child labor, and safe workplaces. She joined his campaign team and worked hard to get him elected, even traveling to eleven Southern states on his behalf. But it was an uphill battle. Smith not only spoke with a heavy New York working class accent, but was the first Roman Catholic ever to win the nomination of a major party. Among other conservative and reactionary groups, the Ku Klux Klan made its opposition to Smith dramatically known wherever he campaigned. Speaking in his support, sometimes Frances had eggs and tomatoes thrown at her by opponents in the crowd. Always trying to defuse anger with humor, she complimented some on their aim when they hit their mark.

One rally both Frances and the clan attended in Missouri ended with fistfights between opposing sides, or as Frances put it, "all bedlam broke loose." She and another Democratic spokeswoman had to be ushered to safety. The very air felt threatening.

Frances Perkins, Action Figure

Not only heroic in speaking out in dangerous situations, Frances could also *physically* spring into action when the situation called for it. One moving example occurred when Franklin Roosevelt made his first public speech following his life-threatening battle with polio, which left his legs almost completely paralyzed.

He was appearing at the 1924 Democratic convention to nominate his friend Al Smith for President. It was important that as a working class Catholic, Smith have the support of a prominent, well-respected Protestant politician from an upper-class background. FDR, crippled by polio, had worked hard to build up his strength and recover as much use of his legs as possible, but would never again be able to walk unassisted. Though he wore leg braces, he still needed a crutch on one side and his teenaged son on the other to assist him to the steps of the platform. Then with a second crutch he started for the speaker's stand. It was a struggle, and a slow process, while the audience watched, holding their breath. When he got there, he handed off the crutches to his son, took a deep breath, and gave the audience a wide, dazzling grin. The crowd cheered. He could not remove a hand from the lectern to wave back, but his smile made up for it. He spoke clearly and vigorously. Only Frances, who had a good vantage point, observed the extent of Roosevelt's physical struggle. His hands trembled as they gripped the podium and she knew that supporting himself must be agonizing. She also knew how important it was for him to appear capable and in control, if he was to have any future as a politician. She began to think of the stressful moment when Roosevelt's speech would end and he would be faced again with the challenge of walking, with everyone witnessing his handicap at every step.

Then she had an idea. She knew the male politicians around the speaker would never think of it. She whispered her idea to the women around her. The moment FDR finished speaking and the applause began, they rushed up to the platform and stood between him and the convention audience. As he turned away on crutches, he appeared to be swamped by supporters congratulating him. Their moving sea of skirts and hats shielded him from view. In fact, the maneuver worked so well that it was used in future appearances.

It was a small action, but one that spoke volumes of her sensitivity and empathy. Most people cannot quickly think of the right thing to do in a sticky situation. It may come to them a day, a week, or a month later. Frances acted on her idea within seconds of seeing the need to aid her friend.

In another case, an insurance company refused to pay a worker who'd had a blow to the head on a construction job. He'd been unable to work after the accident, for his brain injury caused him to become deranged. In court, the insurance company tried to claim that the man had mental problems *before* the injury occurred. But Frances disagreed, and ordered compensation be paid. When the company still dragged its feet about paying, the delusional man believed it to be Miss Perkins' fault. He stormed into her office one day with a knife. Unable to find her, he attacked the first person he found and slashed his throat, fortunately not quite deep enough to be fatal. The victim was the lawyer for the insurance company. Emerging from the restroom, Frances saw a man with a knife, and another man bleeding from the neck. Again, she sprang into action, catching the victim just before he hit the floor. She instantly took charge of the situation issuing orders to call for an ambulance and the police. Although the attacker was taken to a mental hospital, Frances, always empathetic, saw to it that his family was paid his workman's compensation.

Smith's presidential campaign continued to be an uphill battle. She knew before election day that Smith would lose to the Republican candidate, Herbert Hoover, and she was right. It was a crushing and humiliating blow for her friend, Al Smith.

On the same night, however, to the surprise of many, Franklin Delano Roosevelt was elected to the office Smith had vacated: governor of the great state of New York.

Ready To Tackle Big Things

When FDR took over the reins as governor, he sat with his predecessor, Smith.

"Franklin, I've got an important piece of advice for you. There's one person in my administration you should definitely hold on to. It's my Chair of the Industrial Board."

FDR just grinned. He had been a Frances fan since the early days of her bulldog lobbying tactics in Albany and already had bigger plans for her in this new administration.

"I'll do that, Al, if she'll have me!"

He made Frances the first woman cabinet member in New York history, the Industrial Commissioner, head of the entire state Department of Labor. It was ten years earlier that Smith had first appointed her to serve on the Commission, bringing on a storm of protest. This time labor leaders and manufacturers cheered her appointment. In fact, she was thrown a huge party. Two weeks after her swearing in, 800 people gathered to honor Perkins at a lavish lunch in a historic New York City hotel, the Astor. Frances spoke humbly, giving credit to the many people in her life who had contributed to her "knowledge… information… and character." She promised three things: to meet problems with intelligence and courage, to be candid about the state of labor throughout New York and the entire country, and to share the whole truth at all times.

In fact, she had been reluctant to accept the post, having enjoyed the hands-on work of being a commissioner, but she again was reminded of her grandmother's advice that "If anybody opens a door, one should always go through." It would be hard constantly traveling back and forth from Albany to New York City to be with her husband and young daughter. In the end, the deciding factor was that Governor Roosevelt gave her assurances. He agreed to support her every effort to reduce workers' hours, improve safety codes and conditions, improve on compensation to injured workers, restrict child labor, and do away with sweatshops. Thus reassured, she accepted his offer.

Roosevelt was now very different from the self-confident, self-assured, wealthy, and athletic young man she had first met in 1910. After all, he had barely survived an attack of polio (then called infantile paralysis), which had struck him at age 39. As Frances later wrote in her best-selling book *The Roosevelt I Knew,* "He escaped death by a narrow margin and then, through the dynamic force of his courage, he slowly began to fight his way back to health." His disability had changed him in many ways. Now she found him much kinder and more approachable. Frances considered his return to politics a near miracle, as he was almost completely confined to a wheelchair. Yet he'd had a great deal of time for reading, reflecting, and coming to understand the less privileged citizens of his country. He had new empathy for them. He committed himself to helping improve their lot. Frances wrote,

The man emerged completely warmhearted, with humility of spirit and with a deeper philosophy. Having been to the depths of trouble, he understood the problems of people in trouble... he had developed faith in the capacity of troubled people to respond to help and encouragement.

The two were destined to become close allies. Franklin and Frances saw eye to eye on the need for the labor reform movement. Working together on a daily basis, they forged a close friendship and partnership that would last right up until FDR's death in 1945. He trusted her sound research, grasp of facts, her ideas, honesty, and integrity.

Chapter 12

Hard Times: The Great Depression

The United States economy seemed to be booming in 1929. The nation's wealth had doubled during the 1920's. Industrialists were amassing huge fortunes by building railroads, manufacturing steel, and drilling oil. Americans were buying homes, with the help of mortgages, as never before. They were ordering their first automobiles and purchasing new labor-saving devices like refrigerators and washing machines. Almost all of it was on credit, known as the installment plan. All that was needed was a small down-payment and the rest could be paid in "easy monthly installments." America seemed to be living high on the good life in the midst of prosperity. The nation was enjoying the post-World War I freedom of "the Roaring Twenties."

Frances was not so confident. She was beginning to see negative signs, cracks in the foundation of the economy. Farmers were having a bad year, due to drought and falling food prices, and many were unable to make mortgage payments on their farms. She found a disturbing trend toward unemployment in many sectors. Textile workers in the center of the industry, New York, were not sharing in the prosperity. She knew that nationwide there were millions of factory workers out of a job. Friends she expressed concerns to shrugged and said things like, "We've always had unemployment, just like we've always had death and taxes. Just look at real estate. (Prices were sky high.) Look at the stock market!" It was indeed booming. People who could afford to "play the market" were getting rich buying and selling stocks. But at the same time, hundreds of banks were being forced to shut their doors. They had granted too many loans that were not being paid off. Frances knew from her studies in economics and the figures coming out of her department that the wild, upward spiraling boom couldn't last.

An economic slowdown, or mild recession, began in the summer, with buying and selling falling off. By September, just months after President Herbert Hoover's inauguration, investors began to sell off their stocks, their shares in businesses. Frances was not the only one to sense doom on the horizon.

Meanwhile, she worked to revamp and revitalize the free public employment service in her state, and within one year they placed tens of thousands of people in jobs. But it was not enough. Masses of investors began selling off shares of public stocks with inflated values.

On a day in late October which came to be known as Black Friday, the stock market crashed. People panicked as the market saw the greatest ever tidal wave of stock selling, a deluge that drowned bankers and investors alike. Millions of shares became worthless overnight, in addition to all those bought "on margin," or with borrowed money.

The Crash was a fatal blow that would take almost a decade to fully recover from. The period that followed was known as The Great Depression, and almost all Americans suffered from it in one way or another. It proved to be the worst failure of an economy in the history of the industrial world.

Frances Challenges the President

Several weeks after the crash, Frances was shocked to see a well-dressed woman in New York City rummaging in a garbage can for something to feed her family. On other blocks she saw more women carrying paper bags and doing the same thing. She was horrified.

The figures on her desk that morning from Herbert Hoover, the president, shocked her even more. He claimed that America was just experiencing a temporary slump. Frances knew otherwise. When the stock market collapsed, people's savings were wiped out, but that was not all. The crash had started a chain reaction that broke down the economy everywhere. Credit was now so tight that people whose banks had closed were terrified to part with what cash they had. How could a store, factory, or restaurant stay open when no one would buy? Workers were fired by the tens of thousands. Cars and appliances bought on credit were re-possessed, and worse yet, people could not make the payments on their homes, which were being foreclosed and taken back by the mortgage lenders at alarming rates. Many people were forced to move in with relatives, two or even three generations together. Others crowded into small, shared apartments. Yet here was the president quoting federal labor statistics and telling the country business was improving!

Frances was not a woman to sit still in the face of glaringly false information. She studied the latest report she had from her own state labor bureau and called her secretary in. Then she dictated a short statement and instructed her assistant to send it to the newspapers. She went about her work day, not giving her initiative much thought.

Frances had taken a very gutsy action. She had contradicted the president! When the evening newspaper came out, it was a big shock. She thought there'd be a little piece containing her correction of facts printed on a back page. Instead, a front-page headline led with her name! Her statement had pointed out that in the 2,000 or so factories in New York, unemployment had been steadily *rising* for the past few months, and that the situation was unlikely to be different in other states. The newspapers added that the New York Labor Commissioner was directly challenging the president's accuracy!

Horrified, she realized that she had made a grave mistake by not consulting FDR first. She was sure everyone would assume that the challenge had come from him, not her, and that it might hurt his chances if he ran in the next presidential election.

With fear and anxiety, she called her boss first thing in the morning ready with profuse apologies. Her first question was, "Are you going to kill me, or fire me?" His response was a deep laugh. "Apologize! For what? I say *bully* for you. I think your statement was an excellent one… I say keep up the good work!" "Bully" was the favorite adjective of Teddy Roosevelt for anything he was enthusiastic about. His cousin Franklin had adopted it.

As the depression worsened everywhere, Frances and Franklin charged ahead, introducing legislation for unemployment insurance and pensions to help workers survive. Roosevelt sent Frances to England to study their unemployment situation and gather ideas for new bills.

As Bad As It Gets

People were desperate in the U.S. as the depression stretched from months into years. Things got about as bad as they could. Throngs of formerly successful, self-sufficient workers had been unemployed so long that they survived only by standing in long breadlines or queues at soup kitchens for a little free food. NO HELP WANTED signs were posted everywhere they looked for jobs. Homelessness increased daily. About one in every six homes were lost through foreclosure, as banks seized them. Former executives were among the unemployed who sold pencils or apples on New York street corners in a desperate attempt to feed their families. How could they afford to buy the apples to sell? According to Frances, "Some kind-hearted man who had a surplus of apples — because the farmers were in this depression too — thought of getting rid of the apples he couldn't sell by giving them to the unemployed."

In England, they had mandatory unemployment insurance as early as 1911, but Americans, including FDR and Perkins felt that the payouts were little better than charity. In fact, in the U.K., they called it "the dole." Frances told her boss that doling out money to the unemployed was "The quickest way to break a man's spirit. People want to work for their money." The governor was in strong agreement. So instead, with FDR's support, she redirected the New York State Employment Service so that it became a clearinghouse — a central resource — for job seekers across the state. She even added a "Junior Jobs" division for boys and girls under seventeen so they too could help their families survive.

New York also became the first state to provide funding for relief, forming a Stabilization of Industry committee. In 1931 and 1932 the Roosevelt administration provided close to a million beds and nearly four million meals using state money.

But in such a dire crisis, there were simply not enough jobs. By 1933, the height of the depression, eleven thousand banks had failed, wiping out the life savings of millions of Americans. Half of all families were now living below the poverty level, without the income necessary for survival. Fifteen to eighteen million were jobless nationwide. That represented a quarter of all workers. Some people were starving, though many scratched the earth to plant vegetables that could help sustain them.

Frances was convinced that only a federal government mass recovery program could avert disaster nationwide. But President Hoover stood firm that it was up to private charities to help the unemployed. He believed that government should not intervene in the economy, create jobs, or provide relief.

As millions became homeless, many people lived and begged on the streets. Others banded together to set up "shantytowns" — homeless encampments. They put up tents, shacks, huts or whatever could provide a bit of shelter, on empty land all over the country. Some lived under railroad bridges to keep the rain and snow off. Many were situated near free soup kitchens. Sometimes old newspapers served as blankets. Bitter over the conditions they were forced to live in, people called their small enclaves "Hoovervilles," believing the president was to blame.

And then a ray of hope emerged out of Frances's despair. The Democratic Party was encouraging Roosevelt to run against Hoover in 1932! She was convinced that he would accept his party's nomination. When he did, he campaigned in 38 out of the 48 states. Voters were almost as hungry for hope and change as they were for food. When he pledged a "New Deal" to help the forgotten at the bottom of the economic pyramid, people listened and grew hopeful. Frances was confident he would win. He was running against President Hoover, who had become the very symbol of the Great Depression.

Roosevelt won in a landslide. Americans were praying for something dramatically new to rescue the country from the brink of collapse.

Chapter 13
Madam Secretary

The Interview

Franklin Delano Roosevelt would be the last president to be inaugurated in March, instead of January. Late in February, 1933, Frances got the call. Would she meet the President-elect in his home in New York City?

She called her close friend Mary Dewson, a Roosevelt insider and confidant, who said, "Sure, I know what it's about. You do too. Don't be such a baby, Frances, you do the right thing. I'll murder you if you don't!" Frances was never "a baby," but had reasons to hesitate. Friends had been hinting to Perkins for weeks that she'd likely be FDR's choice for the Secretary of Labor. Behind the scenes, numerous organizations, and some individuals, including Mary Dewson, had been organizing letter writing campaigns urging him to appoint Perkins. Even the President's wife, Eleanor Roosevelt, was pushing for Frances. To boost her confidence and encourage her to accept, Dewson said, "You can do it as nobody else can." Then to add a bit of pressure as well as historical perspective she added, "You owe it to the women… you must step forward… otherwise generations might pass before a woman is asked again. Too many people count on what you do." Frances later commented, "I had more sense of obligation to do it for the sake of other women… It might be that the door would close on them and (they) wouldn't have the chance."

Still agonizing over the decision, Frances asked the opinion of an Episcopal bishop she knew. After two days of reflection, she received his lengthy and eloquent letter. It praised Frances's commitment, gifts, and experience. But perhaps his most persuasive words were, "I really believe it is God's own call. If it is, you can't refuse… He will help you to see it through." The bishop appreciated the sacrifice that would be called for, adding, "There would be no distinction in that office did it not carry with it a crushing burden or responsibility."

Still she came prepared with her excuses. Frances had struggled mightily with the very concept of becoming part of a presidential administration. She had her family to think about. Her husband continued to need hospitalization on and off, sometimes for months, and required a stable, familiar routine at home in between; her daughter, Susanna, was happy in her school in New York. She also feared the publicity that could bear down on the entire family. Frances prized her own privacy, and felt the need to defend her husband and child from the public glare. Commuting from NYC to Albany by train and back every week had been hard enough. Washington was considerably further. In addition, she felt fulfilled as New York's industrial commissioner, and had been ensured by the Governor-elect that her job was secure. Yes, she needed to earn a good wage, but in fact had been approached numerous times with offers of jobs in private business and industry that would have paid a good deal more than a government position.

Of course, FDR offered her the cabinet position of Secretary of Labor. Her first response, after thanking him for the honor, was to protest that she was not the right person for the job, not being from "labor's ranks," that is, a union leader. FDR just scoffed at that.

So Frances told him, "If I took the post I would want to do a great many things you probably would not agree with." It was both a challenge and an all-or-nothing gamble. But her list was ready. She made it clear that she would be unable to accept unless he vowed to back all of her desired initiatives. The items on her list included:

- Immediate and direct relief to the unemployed;
- Public works: a government created and funded program of new jobs to give honest, meaningful work to the unemployed;
- A law or amendment to the Constitution ending child labor forever;
- Laws setting maximum hours and minimum wages;
- A federal employment service like the one she had set up in New York;
- Unemployment insurance;
- Old age insurance to give workers future security;
- Programs to help each state set up effective labor departments;
- A complete reorganization of the Bureau of Labor Statistics;

- A reform of the Bureau of Immigration;

Also on her list was universal health care so that no one in America would go untreated when ill or injured.

The President-elect and Frances had friendly give and take discussions around several items on her agenda, but also interruptions, resistance, and a little arguing.

Finally, Frances waved her notes and asked him, "Are you sure you want these things done? Because you don't want me for Secretary of Labor if you don't."

He didn't have to ponder the question. FDR's response was, "Yes. I'll back you."

She accepted, pending only a talk with her husband. At the sanitarium in New York the next day, Paul requested only that he not have to move to Washington and that she come home to New York every weekend. She promised.

The president announced the appointment one day later. Generally, there was approval. Only William Green, the president of one of the largest unions, the American Federation of Labor, blasted it.

Inauguration

Few new appointees to the federal government ever had a more chaotic or confusing first two days in Washington than Frances did. Roosevelt had only finished appointing his cabinet at the very end of February. The inauguration was March 4th. And of course, the country was in chaos. Almost nothing had been done to prepare for the transition to a new administration, or to manage the arrival of the new cabinet members in the capital.

Frances couldn't even find a hotel room for herself and her daughter without appealing to an old friend who knew a hotel owner. She described the train station they arrived in as chaotic, with throngs of Republicans leaving and Democrats arriving. Streets and even sidewalks were jam-packed. No car had been sent for them. Unable to find a taxi, they walked a mile to the hotel in the cold, carrying their luggage.

That night a phone call alerted her that she needed to be at a church service with Roosevelt for all incoming cabinet members the next morning. Again, they got to the church on foot. The inauguration was scheduled for right afterwards, on Capitol Hill. More experienced cabinet appointees had arranged for cars to transport them. Frances, being new in Washington, had not. One other cabinet member was in the same predicament, with no cabs available. At last Frances managed to flag down a citizen who agreed to drive them to the Capitol building. Once in sight of it, they were barred by a policeman from entering the grounds. Everyone climbed out and began to run uphill! Frances, of course, had on high heels, making this challenging. To reach the reviewing stand, she and Henry Wallace, the new Agriculture Secretary, had to duck under ropes and run to the far side. They made it just in time to see Roosevelt place his hand on the Bible and take the oath of office.

Later, she said of the president's inaugural speech that "It was a revival of faith." He was bluntly truthful about the crisis, but gave a stirring, challenging, and resoundingly optimistic message, including a phrase that has echoed down through history: "The only thing we have to fear is fear itself."

That night she found herself waiting in a very long, slow-moving line to enter the White House for a big inaugural night dinner. Fortunately, FDR's private secretary spotted her and explained that cabinet members could use the White House's front entrance. She and Susanna were then escorted to the President. A little later, upstairs, the Supreme Court Chief Justice arrived to swear in each cabinet member in turn. Frances came last, her office, the Labor Department, being the most recently added to the cabinet.

Later that evening, just minutes after Frances had arrived at an inaugural ball in her new gown, a messenger from the President came to tell her that she was requested at the White House. FDR didn't want to waste a minute getting down to work. The lights were to stay on late there many a night as the New Deal and its warriors launched into emergency action to attack the Great Depression on all fronts.

The only people in the Labor Department to welcome her were the women from the Children's Bureau and Women's Bureau who stayed on. The outgoing Labor Secretary, a Mr. Doak, made no contact whatsoever with his successor, though welcoming and offering guidance to one's successor upon the start of a new administration was customary.

Cockroaches and Crooks

Before she could tackle any critical agenda actions, Frances discovered that the Labor Department needed some serious cleaning up. Though they were reportedly almost as large as mice, the cockroaches proved to be the easier task, taking merely a couple of weeks of roach poison. Three decades later, she would make President John F. Kennedy laugh as she told her tale of finding cockroaches in the desks, holding her thumb and index finger apart to show how big they were.

Frances quickly learned that Secretary Doak's main focus in the Bureau of Immigration, then part of the Labor Department, had been to track down and deport immigrant aliens. His team of investigators was led by a man named Garsson. They and their squad were guilty of "shakedowns," threatening people with deportation if they didn't pay them off. Their common practice was raiding the homes of suspected aliens, without a warrant, and throwing the residents in jail. Usually the terrorized victims turned out to be either legal aliens or citizens. This was Garsson and Doak's "secret service squad," an "internal spy system," as described by Frances. It was dedicated to getting rid of "unwanted foreigners" through scare tactics. The squad wanted to "keep American jobs for Americans"— as if America were not a nation made up of immigrants!

The two culprits knew their days were numbered under Frances's administration. She had intentionally cut the money budgeted for their operations. But before she could actually fire them, she caught them red-handed.

It was only a few nights into her term when she came back to the office to finish up some work. She thought she'd have the building to herself, but heard voices upstairs. When she asked the night guard, an elderly gentleman, to take her up in the elevator, she heard men's voices coming from the fourth floor. Getting out, she asked him to remain and hold the elevator. She knew the situation could be dangerous, but persisted. She confronted the crooks. There was Garsson with his partners in crime, raiding the file cabinets, piling up papers they wanted to steal. When Frances calmly asked what they were doing, Garsson lied that he was merely cleaning out personal belongings and letters. Frances didn't buy it. She told them to leave at once, taking nothing with them, and that the staff would help them remove what was rightfully theirs the next day.

Garsson's glare was threatening. Likely the documents he was after would have been used to blackmail others and erase evidence of his crimes. It was a tense moment, but Frances stood her ground. As the man put on his coat, she demanded the keys. The next day she had all the locks changed, including the ones on the file cabinets.

Frances had a bit of fun in her first press conference, announcing that she had ousted the shady operators. She added, "It's in our family tradition." As the papers and magazines reported, her Revolutionary War patriot ancestor James Otis had also exposed and denounced government officials, the British, for unlawful searches without a warrant. It took over a decade, but Garsson and his chief accomplice, his brother, were eventually convicted of federal fraud and bribery.

Another priority action she took was to immediately do away with the separate lunchrooms she found in the Labor Department office building, one for white and one for black workers. Such segregated facilities were still common in the nation, including in the capital, but Frances was not about to allow them. Not until over three decades later were all "Whites Only" facilities banned by law. Frances simply knew that segregation was wrong and acted to correct it in her department.

The new Labor Secretary also made it a special point to help black workers, whose rate of unemployment was much higher than whites'. She made sure the new Federal Employment Service could not discriminate, or favor white applicants for jobs. When she hired the Labor Department's first black American to serve in an executive position, as a special advisor, he fondly recalled years later that she had welcomed him with a firm handshake, saying, "Mr. Oxley, we are awfully glad to have you join our family."

Frances Perkins not only reorganized the Federal Employment Service, but set up free employment agencies throughout the country. Within the first four years this made it possible for over 19 million Americans to find jobs.

The same month she was sworn in, Frances was honored in New York City with a formal Testimonial Dinner to celebrate her astonishing appointment as the first Madam Secretary. This time 1,500 people attended; nine of them praised her in speeches. Among them was Eleanor Roosevelt, the president's wife. When Frances's own turn at the microphone came, she was, as ever, humble. And witty. She was glad that her "beloved daughter" was in the audience as "it has always been a matter of negotiation between us as to whether or not she should override my decisions."

Before finishing she thanked all the workers who, during her years as an investigator and commissioner, taught her about life in the world of labor, the "men and women who have no work, no wages, and very little to eat." Ever the feminist, she thanked those who came before: "The whole procession of all the women who have tried during these hundreds of years, the women who made life better for women… who have opened doors for us… I want to be worthy of them."

At her first cabinet meeting, she was very nervous, and fearful that a roomful of men might find her too talkative. So she simply sat and listened. But after all the other department secretaries had spoken about their priorities, the President said, "Frances, don't you want to say something?" It was like being called on in class on the first day in a new school. Imagine how it must feel to be the first woman cabinet secretary in history and have eleven men, at least one smoking a cigar, all turn and stare at you! She knew she had to say something, and later wrote, "I didn't want to, but I knew I had to… my colleagues looked at me with tense curiosity. I think some weren't sure I *could* speak." She kept it short, hoping to end her comments within one minute. She mentioned a public works initiative being a priority, and having called labor leaders to a conference to gather suggestions on relieving unemployment.

Some months later Frances met the wife of another cabinet member who confided that the night of the first cabinet meeting she'd asked her husband this question: "What was Frances Perkins like, and what did she say?" The wife said his response was along the lines of, "Well… I dunno, but she spoke up clear, said it short and simple and then stopped. I think she's all right!"

The First Hundred Days

Team Frances and Franklin were not working at the White House on inauguration night to make a good impression, but because the need for action was so critical. As Frances put it, "Banks were collapsing throughout the nation. Relief stations were closing down for lack of funds. Hunger marchers were on the move protesting. Food riots were becoming more common. Crime, born of the need for food and the necessities of life was on the upsurge." In her recorded *Reminiscences* decades later, she recalled that the new administration was "improvising under a terrible pressure of poverty, distress, despair."

After studying ideas, proposals, and programs in the thousands from experts and organizations, Frances testified repeatedly before Congress, explaining various plans and approaches. By the end of the first 100 days, a record number of bills, fifteen pieces of major legislation, had been passed, all in an effort to end the Great Depression.

FDR had been inaugurated almost at the very hour the banking crisis peaked. First one state, then others, and then on inauguration morning, the New York banks, had closed due to the nationwide banking panic, forced into closing by "runs" on the bank in which masses of customers demanded to withdraw all their savings. To stem the tide, FDR called a "bank holiday" of four days which closed all remaining U.S. banks along with the stock exchange. Frances knew that he did this to rescue the life savings of the American people. Then he called Congress into session to deal with the economic crisis. In just four days in office, the President had a bill on his desk to sign. The legislation put all banks under the supervision of the government. Only those in sound condition could reopen, and once open, the government would give them protection by backing up their assets with Federal Reserve notes. It worked. In just a couple of weeks, the panic runs were over and 1,500 banks were back in business.

Launching a New Deal for America

Frances was on the front lines of the action, working on nearly every bit of it, which included numerous items on her wish list. A majority of the New Deal programs were initiated and largely implemented by her. Some of them had impacts which are still felt today. Among the top hits of the agenda were programs like the CCC, FERA, and the TVA. They sound a bit like alphabet soup, but they brought America back from the brink of collapse. Let's look at what a few stood for:

FERA was the Federal Emergency Relief Administration. It addressed the most urgent needs of the poor like medicines, blankets, soup kitchens, and employment agencies.

The CCC was the Civilian Conservation Corps, and Frances Perkins pioneered its creation. It offered young men a dollar a day (considered generous at that time) for working at jobs that improved our forests and national parks. Some projects involved stocking lakes and rivers with billions of fish, building campgrounds, and planting trees. They even restored some historic battlefields. In addition to wages, the government provided them with food, clothes and medical care. Many national sites today display plaques in honor of the lasting accomplishments of this huge corps of formerly unemployed men. Many of the CCC workers were black men, and over 88,000 Native Americans joined. At first the camps were for men only, but with support from Frances Perkins and Eleanor Roosevelt, camps for 8,500 unemployed single women were added.

NIRA stood for the National Industrial Recovery Act, "to act as a shot in the arm for industry," according to Frances. It created codes, or guidelines, for wages, prices, and work conditions. Advisory boards helped businesses stabilize and revive production. The NIRA also prohibited child labor, which provided more employment for heads of families, and guaranteed that workers could organize and form unions for collective bargaining. Though the codes weren't mandatory, companies that signed on could proudly display the Blue Eagle Emblem in their windows. In this way consumers could choose to support businesses who were helping Americans get back on their feet. What's more, she felt, it brought about "the revival of the American spirit."

The WPA, or Works Progress Administration, was the agency Frances considered the top factor in the recovery. It gave jobs created by the government to unemployed men and teenagers. The WPA built bridges, roads, airports, public buildings, and parks, in addition to nearly 75 percent of the new schools in the country. Many are still in use today. Once workers had an income, everyone benefitted. For instance, the farmers could buy new tractors made in a factory, and supply the grocers, who now had produce to sell, and customers with money to purchase it. "With one dollar for public works, you have created four dollars' worth of national income," Frances observed.

Besides construction, the WPA gave unemployed artists jobs such as painting murals, most still on view today. The idea came from Frances's daughter, after Susanna spoke with the director of the Museum of Modern Art in New York. Both mother and daughter had always loved art, and often pursued drawing and painting as a pastime. But in 1934 the WPA had only created jobs involving building and fixing things. Susanna was so determined that the program include artists that after calling her mother, she arrived in Washington to push the idea, which Frances at first rebuffed. But Susanna was a determined young woman of eighteen and pleaded her case. She said that most public buildings such as libraries and post offices were dreary places, which artists could enliven by painting murals on the walls.

In her biography of FDR over a decade later, Frances was too modest to admit that the idea came from her own daughter, writing that "a young girl who was related to a cabinet member persuaded her reluctant parent to take it up with the President." Thus ended the nagging. To her surprise, FDR was immediately receptive to the idea. He said, "Why not? Surely there must be some public places where paintings are wanted." He realized it would be a waste of talent to have artists work on a construction crew for relief, when they could be creating something of lasting beauty. The first artist Frances's team approached was "just ecstatic" to learn that the government realized that people in the arts, too, needed relief work. Buildings being constructed in the capital were among the first to be decorated. To select the artists, a competition was launched. Each artist was asked to send a painting of their proposed project. When they all arrived, a showing of them was hung in Washington. Frances found it extremely impressive. She hatched the idea of framing and permanently hanging the paintings. After the White House had first choice, 100 others were selected for the walls of the Department of Labor. Frances was delighted.

The Works Progress Administration also paid writers to create guides to historical sites. It gave jobs to actors, too. For example, it sponsored an acclaimed major production of Shakespeare's *Macbeth* in Harlem, New York, with an all-black cast. Frances said in her *Reminiscences,* "The entire WPA project was very imaginative. They found work for archaeologists, research workers, historians." Everyone was paid the same: $15 per week. It was not a lot, but made it possible for thousands of families to survive. Those who had no skills or prior work experience, many of them women, received training.

The TVA (Tennessee Valley Authority) employed men to build dams, which helped farmers, prevented floods and created important sources of hydroelectric power.

One more alphabet soup agency Perkins created was the DLS, the Division of Labor Standards, to help all the states improve working conditions, including health and safety for workers. It was the first time that state governments had received direct help from a Secretary of Labor. Frances made numerous programs and conferences available. The DLS even offered training courses for factory inspectors, and itself investigated hazardous work places. At one, they discovered a tragedy. Five hundred men had died from the lung disease silicosis while working in a dust-filled tunnel or mineshaft. 1500 in all were unable to return to work. Without hesitation, Perkins organized the National Silicosis Conference to prevent it from happening again.

The moment the bill to create the CCC had passed in Congress, Frances Perkins went to work on her biggest, proudest, and most lasting legacy, Social Security.

The Birth of Social Security

The intrepid Labor Secretary found time to direct the crafting of Social Security legislation even while holding press conferences, giving interviews, running meetings, writing articles, and traveling. She went by train to numerous cities in order to educate the public, at conferences, in speeches, and over the radio. She had a gift for taking a complex issue and making it clear to everyday Americans, regardless of their educational level. She could put the need for a new bill in human terms and show people just how it would affect their lives.

Their understanding was particularly important when it came to the issue of Social Security. There was bound to be resistance, as Americans had traditionally prized self-reliance. Americans are a proud people, used to standing on their own two feet. If an elderly person did not have savings to live on, he or she would be cared for by their own extended family, or their community. In want of that, there were charities, many sponsored by churches and synagogues, to help out. Nonetheless, for a century, some destitute people went to the "poorhouse, almshouse, or poor farm," basically a bare-bones facility in which to work without wages and wait to die. These institutions had some financial support from towns, counties, and tax revenue, but were demoralizing places in which society's poorest, most vulnerable, and most elderly were forced to live out their lives.

But the grim realities of the Great Depression changed people's perspective on being independent dramatically. Now people realized that a willingness to work was not enough, and that a job loss could lead to dire insecurity, especially when they grew too old to work. FDR told Frances, when he appointed her head of the Committee on Economic Security in 1934, that "From the cradle to the grave every U.S. citizen should be covered by some sort of social insurance program."

The American people had been badly shaken and were ready to listen. As it turned out, so was Congress. When Perkins published her first book, *People at Work*, in 1934, she wrote, "Americans... have learned out of these four years of depression... that what we all need and want is a sense of security... some reliance that life will not be pulled out from under us by some inexplicable situation."

She went to work on the Social Security project, consulting experts of all sorts for advice: professional people with experience, insurance leaders, statisticians and economists. She knew that in addition to crafting a foolproof plan, she would have to convince Congressmen and Senators of the critical need for social insurance. It was a somewhat revolutionary idea, having never been proposed on the federal level before.

She was convinced that the plan must include insurance for both unemployment and old age. She had FDR's vote of confidence. He told her, "I know you will put your back to it more than anyone else and you will drive it through." The biggest challenge was to find a way to pay for the Social Security system that was fully constitutional. The Supreme Court had already struck down the part of the Industrial Recovery Act that imposed codes regulating industries. The administration then had to get Congress to pass legislation to achieve the same ends. Frances did not want her Social Security act to be thrown out by the high court too.

She was struggling with the knotty funding issue when she ran into one of the Supreme Court justices at a social gathering and got "a windfall… accidentally." She confessed to him laughingly that she didn't know how to finance the program since "your Court tells us what the Constitution permits." His response was simple, but perfect. He told her, "The taxing power of the Federal Government, my dear! The taxing power is sufficient for everything you want and need."

And so that is exactly how the Social Security Act was written, and how it still works today. Simply explained, when you get a job, you give your employer your Social Security number. That's how the government keeps track of the credits you earn. On every paycheck you receive you see a box marked "FICA." It stands for the Federal Insurance Contributions Act. It means that this payday will help amass credits which will one day give you cash benefits. On your pay stub you will see 6.2% of your wages set aside for Social Security and 1.45% for Medicare tax. Your employer then matches these for a total of 15.3%. So you and your boss each pay half. It becomes your automatic savings plan. The system is intergenerational. This means that today's workers are helping pay the benefits of current retirees and other beneficiaries. When it's your turn to receive benefits, current workers will be helping pay them. The Social Security Administration calls it "the most successful anti-poverty program in our country's history."

When signed into law in 1935, it gave numerous good and important things to the American people in addition to federal old age benefits. There were grants to the states for unemployment compensation, aid for blind people, dependent children, and the welfare of needy mothers and children. Four years later it was expanded to include survivor benefits, and in 1956, disability benefits were added.

There were still more amendments to Social Security added over the decades to follow.

There were twenty people present at President Roosevelt's signing of this historic bill; the only one not wearing a suit and tie was the person with the vision, brains, and dedication that had made it a reality.

Today at least one out of every six Americans receives benefits from the program. Though most are retired workers and their dependents, many millions more are disabled. Up to 97 percent of citizens 60 and older receive, or will receive, Social Security benefits. For perhaps a third of them, their benefit checks amount to 90 percent of the income they live on. And though Americans tend to take Social Security for granted after all these years, they all, in fact, owe an enormous debt of gratitude to Frances Perkins, whether they know it or not.

The following year, FDR won a second term as President in another landslide.

Labor Battles

As much work as there was to be done inside her offices, Madam Secretary was a hands-on labor leader. Steel was one of the first industries she wrote codes for. She felt she must make sure steel workers knew she was working in their interests. So, she decided to visit some steel factories. In them she could ask questions about wages, safety, and other conditions and get first-hand information. Often, she would talk with workers at lunch in their cafeterias. In at least one, she showed her fun side by "pitching pennies" with the men to see who would buy lunch. Sometimes she'd even talk with them in their homes.

A town called Homestead, in Pennsylvania, had been the scene of a particularly violent dispute between labor and management several decades earlier. In 1933, Frances visited Homestead to discuss New Deal policy. She arranged with the burgess, or mayor, to hold a meeting there in the Hall of Burgesses to meet with aggrieved steelworkers. Frances was about to show her backbone once again. When the meeting, full of officials, press, and workers was underway, Frances heard a great commotion coming from the street and the hall below. A reporter said that the burgess had refused to allow many of the workers in! The burgess told her the men denied entrance were "no good" and "just wanted to make trouble." But

Frances insisted. She knew that if they were not heard, they were *more* likely to make trouble. She respected their right of free speech, and later wrote, "I believed that the burgess was a public officer to whom all citizens of his community were equally important." Not about to back down, she went outside to have a conversation with the assembled group. But the burgess, now with the police in tow, would not give her an inch, shouting that there was a rule against making a speech there.

Perkins replied, "Alright, we will go over to the public park." The burgess, now red in the face, shouted at her, "You can't do that. There is an ordinance against holding meetings in a public park!" At this point most people would have felt defeated, given up, and gone home. Not Frances. She spotted an American flag across the square. Aha, she thought, that must be a post office — Federal Government property! And off she went with the crowd behind her.

Though it was just minutes before closing time, the postmaster agreed to her request. Standing on a chair, she made a little speech about the new codes for steel, and how they could improve the lives and wages of workers. Then she listened as steel workers spoke their minds. Some of the men were angry with current conditions, but she promised their spokesman the opportunity to speak at a public hearing in Washington. The impromptu meeting ended with handshakes all around.

There was a downside to having imposed codes that made it legal for unions to organize. Employers not used to dealing with organized workers were digging in their heels, causing a series of strikes to break out across the country. There was bound to be violence. Frances began to read headlines about riots, people being shot, picket line fights, and even troops being called out.

In the summer of 1934, a truly serious strike reached epic proportions in San Francisco. The longshoremen, who worked at the docks loading and unloading shipments by sea, went on strike. They paralyzed the city by refusing to handle cargo until their demands were met. Soon men in other unions, engineers, firemen and truck drivers also struck, in support of the longshoremen. On July 5th, following fights between strikers and police officers, scores of men were injured seriously and two were left dead. The day came to be called "Bloody Thursday." By Monday, matters were still worsening. This was a crisis!

Unfortunately, FDR was on a ship en route to Hawaii, leaving his Secretary of State, Cordell Hull, in charge. Hull and the Attorney General were both alarmed enough to recommend sending in federal troops to "break this up." Only Frances kept a cool head. She stood up for restraint. She pointed out that the strikers had done nothing much more serious than inconveniencing the community. She was firm that they must send a cable to the President for him to authorize any such action.

She also sent her own private cable to FDR. He thanked her for her frank assessment of the issues… and then gave her complete authority to speak for him. She next issued a public statement which helped to defuse the situation. Within days the strike ended with the ship owners and longshoremen agreeing to settle. She had once again averted bloodshed.

There are too many accomplishments of the first Madam Secretary in the record-breaking twelve years she served under President Roosevelt to include them all in this book. But a few highlights follow:

The Supreme Court struck down the industry codes the National Recovery Act (NRA) had developed, just two years after they were passed. The justices ruled that despite the economic emergency, the President had overstepped his powers, since the lawsuit brought by an industry did not involve interstate commerce. The Constitution allows the federal government to control business between the states, but not within individual states.

It was a blow to the administration, but Frances was prepared. She had sensed that if anything went wrong with the NRA, they had to have a back-up plan. So she pulled out of her drawer two bills she'd drafted earlier and shared them with the President, telling him they would "do everything you and I think important under NRA." The first mandated that anything purchased by the government (the largest customer of most industries) must be made under conditions which included health and safety, a minimum wage, 40-hour week, and an 8-hour day, while it banned child labor. It quickly passed Congress.

The second bill, after being repeatedly rewritten and revised was quite broad. One provision made it illegal to hire a child under sixteen in any industry involving interstate commerce. Another mandated pay for overtime work. It became known as the Wages and Hours Act, or, more commonly, the Fair Labor Standard Act. When it passed (unanimously in the Senate) several in Congress tried to take credit for it. But Frances knew the brains and guts of it were her work, with input from FDR. She didn't need the glory. Ever. She always felt rewarded when something was achieved "for the general good."

No one but Perkins could ever take the credit for getting America to join the International Labor Organization, though. The ILO was begun in order to oversee and improve conditions for workers worldwide. When she attended her first ILO conference in Geneva, Switzerland in 1936, she became the first ever American cabinet member to speak there. Her speech, and her success in getting the U.S. to join, scored many points. One reporter dubbed her "the world's outstanding Secretary of Labor." It turned out to be significant that she had the satisfaction of this recognition, as dark clouds were looming back home.

Chapter 14
Trials and Tribulations

It was never going to be easy to be a ground-breaker. Throughout much of her life Frances paid a steep price for dramatically changing the country while blazing a trail for women yet to come. As capable and dedicated as she was, her career was often a painful uphill battle.

For example, she knew when FDR announced her appointment as Secretary of Labor that there would be resentment. But the prejudice and discrimination which mounted against her went beyond resentment. Naturally it would be important to have good relationships with the top labor leaders of the country's unions. It wouldn't be easy. William Green was president of one of the most powerful organizations, the American Federation of Labor. When she was named to FDR's cabinet, he immediately announced to the public, "We will never be reconciled to her appointment." Another labor spokesman told the press, "We simply will not deal with the lady, that is all." John L. Lewis headed up not only the Congress of Industrial Organizations, but the United Mine Workers. As Frances labored to deal with the knotty issues of industrial strikes plaguing the country, he told a newspaper interviewer, "Madam Perkins is woozy in the head. She doesn't know as much about economics as a Hottentot." (The Hottentots were a primitive South African tribe of hunter-gatherers.)

Whenever she engaged in helping resolve a strike, she dealt with a heap of criticism. Usually business leaders faulted her for not being tough enough. Eventually she felt compelled to defend her approach:

I have been called incompetent (and worse) because I have not prevented strikes... there is a theory that if I were a two-fisted male, I should be able to stop strikes. The accusation that I am a woman is incontrovertible. As for being two-fisted, I'm sure it is unrealistic and lacking in human knowledge to believe that getting tough or cracking down on working people would make things better. I believe that strikes and disputes should be settled by negotiation and mutual agreement.

Perkins and the Press

Handling public relations had been a great challenge for Frances. By nature, she was a very private person. Even some of her closest friends did not know the details of her personal life. Naturally she did not want to talk in public about her marriage or her young daughter. Her husband's mental condition was very painful to her and not a suitable topic for discussion in public. For one thing, there was at that time a feeling of stigma or shame attached to mental illness, which was little understood. What's more, there was still active prejudice against a married woman working at all. She also feared for Susanna's safety. Following the explosive story of famed aviator Charles Lindbergh's baby son's kidnapping and death a year earlier, every wealthy or famous parent was worried. A rash of kidnappings had followed the Lindbergh case.

Yet she was constantly intruded on by reporters. One thing they repeatedly demanded was an explanation of her name: "Why do you call yourself Miss Perkins when you are married and have a daughter?" Naturally, this was not a question she could reply to simply. She quickly learned to dodge reporters whenever possible. It was just the start of a rocky relationship. In *The Roosevelt I Knew* she admitted "my own lamentable lack of instinct for publicity."

Frances always wanted to talk statistics, policy, actions, and solutions. She wanted to give thoughtful and intelligible answers. But as the first woman in a cabinet post, the press and public found her a tantalizing novelty. She grew impatient quickly when hounded with questions that she considered "fluff," more suitable for the "Women's Pages" of the day than for interviewing a cabinet member. Sometimes, when asked something strictly personal, she would respond, "Is that quite necessary?" Reporters were always looking for a "human interest" angle. Some, frustrated at the lack of any juicy content from Frances, took to describing her eyes: "shining more than usual," or "It is her eyes that tell her story. Large and dark and vivid, they take their expression from her mood. If she is amused, they scintillate with little points of light," and so forth.

There were other slights. On one occasion a men-only press club held a dinner in honor of cabinet members. All were invited except Frances. On another occasion one of her fellow cabinet members gave a dinner party. Another wrote, "After dinner the men, all of us being members of the cabinet, went upstairs to smoke and have our coffee. This gave us an opportunity to talk about important national matters." Of course, Frances was expected to stay downstairs and sip her coffee with their wives.

She'd gotten off to a bad start with reporters following her very first appearance before Congress shortly after the inauguration. Trying to appear professional to hide her considerable nervousness, she came off as stiff and official and having a superior attitude. Afterwards, eager for her ordeal to be over with, she'd tried to brush off newsmen (there were as yet few newswomen hired.) As a result, the newspaper accounts called her such things as "blunt," "impatient," and "regal." One reported that she *insisted* on being addressed "Madam Secretary." In fact, she had always requested to be addressed as "Miss Perkins." In revenge for her standoffishness, the papers and public often referred to her as "Madam Perkins" instead.

The negative coverage was counted as "news," and only attracted more reporters. For days, they congregated in her outer office, waiting sometimes an hour or more, hoping for their questions to be answered. They gradually stopped coming. One particular morning there was just one, and he insisted on seeing her. When her secretary, quoting Frances, told him there would be "absolutely no interviews today," he barged into Frances's office. He snapped, "Just let me tell you something... the press can do a lot to help you. And YOU can't do a thing to help the press." And he stomped out.

Frances was not only shocked by his outburst, but genuinely puzzled by it. Instead of brushing off the incident, she pondered it, thinking about her interactions with the press — and lack of them — over the past months. She realized that from their point of view, her treatment of reporters had in fact been shabby. As an honest and just person, she was willing to come face to face with her mistakes and short-comings. She spent an hour reviewing them, remembering all the times reporters had sat wasting time in her outer office, hoping for an interview. She had the frightening feeling that they had completely given up on her.

She knew that good working relationships with the media were important to getting the Labor Department's plans out to the public. She set her mind to mending fences. For the next week she invited small gatherings of newspapermen to join her for dinner or tea. They were wary at first, but came to admit that she was warm, a gracious host, and a very good person.

Reporters began collecting in her waiting room again. Seeing a gaggle of them one morning, she stopped and said she wanted to have a candid chat with them. She began by admitting her flaw: "As some of you may have gathered by now, I don't have much of a flair for public relations." She smiled; they grinned back. She went on to confess, "A mass interview terrifies me. I'm frank to admit, however, that I've been wrong in not understanding that when you are sent to interview somebody… your jobs depend on your getting that news." And then she talked about the Civilian Conservation Corps, or CCC (the big new program looming), and took their questions. Things were considerably better after that.

Impeachment Charges!

Her good nature and new openness to the press was not enough. Some members of Congress came to feel that she was too outspoken and influential. They still criticized that she did not use her husband's name. Keeping one's maiden name after marriage was considered as radical in the mid-1930's as it had been in 1913.

Frances was an anomaly to both her supporters and detractors, a married woman who went by the name "Miss Perkins" and came to Washington without her husband or daughter. Due in large part the high costs of Paul's medical care, and Susanna's private school, she always felt significant financial pressure. She took a small apartment upon arriving in the capital, but soon learned that a degree of hosting was important in government circles. Dinner parties or even afternoon teas were impossible in her apartment.

Help came in the form of an old friend, activist and frequent correspondent, Mary Harriman Rumsey, who was wealthy. Mary owned estates in both nearby Virginia and Long Island, New York, as well as a reasonably spacious home in the Georgetown section of Washington. Mary was an ardent supporter of Frances, and proposed a solution. She urged Frances to share the home, where she'd have her own bedroom, sitting room and office, and contribute to certain household expenses with Mary. Frances gratefully accepted.

Over a period of about seventeen months in 1933 and 1934 the two enjoyed one another's warm friendship, and frequently entertained together, a valuable asset to Frances's career. Tragically, the arrangement came to a sudden halt when Mary, an accomplished equestrienne, died after being thrown from her horse. Frances grieved her friend, and was very soon required to move.

Sadly, false allegations can always arise out of little more than thin air. There are those in our own era who have implied that two women living together, regardless of the circumstances, must be lovers. Some have tried to portray the friends' joint tenancy and fond letters to one another as proof of a sexual liaison. However, the only two individuals still living who knew Frances extremely well are quite certain that this was not the case. They believe Frances was always heterosexual and always faithful to her absent husband.

But in politics there are always opponents ready to backstab, and there has always been what we now call "fake news." Her detractors looked for something with which to undermine her authority. Today we might say they "looked for dirt on Frances." It was an era long before television, the internet, and social media. Instead, what was referred to as "a whispering campaign" began against her.

Someone dug up records of a Russian-born Jewish woman who had married a man named Paul Wilson in 1910. On that flimsy basis they accused Frances of being that woman, and an imposter. Even though the Russian woman was born 12 years later than she was, the campaign against her gained traction. Frances responded with a letter to be shared with anyone questioning her identity. In it she said,

> There were no Jews in my ancestry. If I were a Jew, I would make no secret of it. On the contrary I would be proud to acknowledge it. The utter un-Americanism of such a whispering campaign, the appeal to racial prejudice and the attempt at political propaganda… must be repugnant to all honorable men and women.

In 1938 the House of Representatives launched a committee to delve into "Un-American Activities." It targeted anyone suspected to have ties to Communism or fascism. It took the committee only a few months to declare that hundreds of newspapers and labor unions across the country were communist! It also branded individuals, including one named Harry Bridges. He was one of the labor leaders involved in the big longshoremen's strike Frances had helped resolve by refusing to send federal troops to San Francisco. Bridges was a man she had met in person, and found to be calm and level-headed. But Martin Dies, chairman of the House committee, began pressuring Perkins to have Bridges deported.

She did her homework, but her investigation turned up not a shred of evidence that Bridges had any association with Communism. On the contrary, research showed him to be a hard-working, bill-paying citizen fond of spending his evenings playing the mandolin. When Perkins still refused to deport Bridges, a New Jersey representative in the House introduced a 40-page long Resolution of Impeachment against her in January, 1939. It read, "for failing, neglecting and refusing to enforce the immigration laws."

Frances, of all people, under a cloud of *IMPEACHMENT?!* It was a shock and a stunning blow. She and two members of her staff were charged with "high crimes and misdemeanors in violation of the Constitution," and headlines everywhere blared the news. Imagine how it must have felt. Here was a public servant so dedicated that she regularly worked 14-hour days, and sometimes through the night, to (among other goals) shorten workdays for others. Year after year she had summoned extraordinary stamina and drive to achieve the general welfare of all, never shirking from a task, no matter how thorny or unpopular. She did so at the great personal sacrifice of living apart from her family five days a week. She looked for no praise or publicity. But to be falsely accused before the eyes of the world must have been devastating.

In her characteristic understated way, all she would later say of the whole humiliating ordeal was, "It was extremely painful… it was a terrible winter." All along there had been periodic bad press and even occasional death threats. But 1939 topped all. Now Dies, the chairman of the committee that called for her impeachment, was demanding her resignation. Her mailbox was filled with hate mail. There were some ugly editorials against her. At times she felt like a first century Christian about to be thrown to the lions.

Then as now, public sentiment often seemed to hold sway over hard facts. Sadly, along with anti-Communist rhetoric, anti-immigrant and anti-Jewish prejudice was on the rise. Frances was a person who routinely had stood up for both immigrants and Jews. Individuals and organizations came out against the Secretary of Labor almost daily all that winter. Even some Democrats, including one in the cabinet, pressured Frances to deport Bridges, even though a Court of Appeals had ruled him "undeportable." But President Roosevelt backed his Labor Secretary up, lacking any legal proof of Bridges' guilt. He told her not to worry.

Refuge

FDR's unwavering support helped, but she needed more. Always a spiritual person and regular church member, she now used her faith to help her through this crisis.… She had been privately spending one or two days a month at a retreat for several years. It was an Episcopal convent an hour's train ride away, near Baltimore, Maryland. After confiding in a clergyman, the rector at her Washington church, he recommended she try it. She had told him of the stresses and strains of her job, including the realization that if she failed, it would be viewed as a defeat for women everywhere. The convent community she visited was a small one, out in the country surrounded by woods, with a view of a river. It became a critical refuge in her life. It gave her a chance to get away from the Capital and commune with nature. It gave her the gift of time to think, study, pray, attend small services, and discuss the big ideas behind social legislation with the Reverend Mother there.

The convent imposed a "rule of silence" for all but two hours of every day, and Frances decided, after the noise of the city, and the constant political debates, that,

Silence is one of the most beautiful things in the world… It preserves one from the temptation of the idle word, the fresh remark, the wisecrack, the angry challenge, the hot-tempered reaction, the argument about nothing, the foolish question, the unnecessary noise of the human clack-clack.

Her convent visits had helped keep her stressful life in balance until now. But following the Resolution of Impeachment, she began to attend church daily to save her sanity. When she told her pastor she was finding it hard to pray for her enemies, he suggested that she pray for those who give false witness to be enlightened. But attacks from Congressman Dies continued; he seemed to be raising an army of critics against her, and some members of the press followed. It was hard to withstand. She had escaped to the family homestead in Maine for a few quiet days or a little vacation whenever possible every year, but now she longed for the sanctuary and privacy of The Brick House keenly.

Throughout it all, she kept to her routine. Almost invariably she was in her office by early morning, working up until a brief break for a little supper. Then she would often return and work until midnight or later. She also continued addressing groups on important legislation, but seldom got through a public session without being asked whether she was secretly related to Bridges or a communist herself. Some asked if her daughter Susanna was married to Bridges!

Others in FDR's administration had been accused from time to time of being socialists and communists, and labeled Jewish when they were not. But according to Eleanor Roosevelt in a letter, "Miss Perkins was the easiest victim." Dies apparently felt that this sensationalized political attack would help get him nominated for President. Frances thought Dies was obsessed with the notion that immigrants were undesirables.

She had confronted the charges courageously, head-on, by almost immediately volunteering to appear and answer them. But the Judiciary Committee which would run the hearing repeatedly put her off. The wait seemed endless. She wanted a full public hearing in order to fully clear her name. Instead they voted that it would be private. Not until February 7th and 8th did she get to testify as "the accused" and then appear before the committee as a voluntary witness. She was not quite alone, as an attorney for the Labor Department accompanied her. She told him she felt like Joan of Arc on her way to the stake to be burned.

She brought with her a carefully prepared and detailed statement; copies were given to reporters, who were then dismissed. A long and intense questioning period — or interrogation — followed, much of it in angry, accusatory tones. She remained calm, and gave her answers thoroughly, and without having to keep the inquisitors waiting. Her conduct and demeanor earned her a private compliment from the chairman when the ordeal was over. Then there was nothing to do but wait, while the committee heard other testimony and took its time. Not until 44 days later was there a response. The wait must have felt interminable. The committee's statement came two months to the day after the Impeachment Resolution was issued. It read as follows: "After careful consideration of all the evidence in this case, this Committee is unanimous in its opinion that sufficient facts have not been presented to warrant impeachment by the House."

The resolution was dismissed and the nightmare was finally over.

Unfortunately, even the unanimous judgement did not stop the attacks, one of them from a congressman, in a national radio broadcast days later. He lied that "the Secretary of Labor and her associates have been... officially condemned." This public blanket condemnation would prove hard to recover from. The newspapers gave very little space to the committee's *dismissal* of all charges, compared to the huge amount of sensationalized publicity they had given to the *accusations* against her.

Of course, she had her supporters, and a Democratic Congressman who had never met her made a speech two days later on the floor of the House, defending Frances. He decried that "a case which thundered so long... has dwindled to almost less than a whisper," in the press. He angrily emphasized that "this abortive attempt to destroy the first woman ever to have the honor of a seat in the cabinet" was over.

25,000 copies of his speech were distributed by the Department of Labor and the Democratic National Committee. It wasn't much, but it was some consolation, on the heels of such devastating publicity over the span of half a year. There continued to be attacks, but also admirers who spoke out or wrote testimonials on her behalf. The Secretary of State she served with wrote in his memoirs, "Miss Perkins has never received the full credit she deserves for her ability and public services. She was unusually able, very practical, and brought vision and untiring energy to her work."

The attention of the press and the public turned from the Labor Secretary to the war in Europe before the year was out. After invasions by Adolf Hitler's armies, most of Europe was at war. The U.S. remained neutral, but quietly supported the war efforts of Great Britain and its allies. Many people believed the U.S. could not stay out of the war for long.

Frances also played a major role in responding to the crisis caused by Nazi Germany's persecution of Jews. She is credited with helping save hundreds of thousands of refugees. Once immigrants who had visas arrived in the United States, the Immigration Service of the Department of Labor had the job of deciding whether to admit them or not. In 1933, the Bureau of Immigration's work dominated the Department of Labor, consuming three-quarters of its budget. Although some in Congress and the State Department opposed her, Secretary Perkins delved into ways to relax immigration regulations to aid Jews and others who were fleeing Nazi persecution.

After the nationwide terror attack on Jewish people across Germany in 1938, she helped convince President Roosevelt to combine German and Austrian quotas to increase the odds of immigration for Jews, though it still remained very difficult for them to gain admittance to the United States.

President Roosevelt permitted Perkins to extend the visas of some fifteen thousand Jewish people already in the United States. He backed Perkins against State Department opposition, explaining that in view of the dangers awaiting them if they returned to the Europe, it would be a "cruel and inhumane thing to compel them to leave here."

Some members of the cabinet and Congress claimed that Perkins once again was not enforcing immigration regulations strictly enough and was potentially endangering the country by admitting refugees with radical political views who might become anti-American agitators. Her stand on Jewish immigration was part of the background against which they had attempted to remove her from office in 1939. The Bridges case gave them another way to bring false charges against her. By May 1940, Roosevelt had become convinced that spies and people who might sabotage the war efforts could indeed be entering the country along with legitimate refugees. Nonetheless, Frances continued to apply quotas as liberally as possible. Once the U.S. was at war, the President, by executive order, transferred the Bureau of Immigration to the Department of Justice. Immigration decisions were now out of Frances's hands.

Altogether, between 180,000 and 225,000 mostly Jewish refugees entered the U.S., mostly thanks to Frances Perkins.

A Third Term

In a major break with tradition, FDR decided to run to be the first three-term president. At first shocked, Frances decided that given his proven ability to lead in times of crisis, another term would be a good thing. She also believed that only FDR could and would continue to build on the important foundation of New Deal legislation.

The Republicans nominated Wendell Willkie, a very competent and experienced opponent. But Willkie made a blunder. In one of his speeches, he boasted that if he won, he would appoint a new labor secretary.... And "it would not be a woman." Apparently his overwhelmingly male crowd cheered. FDR some time afterwards asked Frances, "Why did he have to insult every woman in the United States? It will make them mad, and lose him votes." Frances smiled. She knew all about it, having already received hundreds of letters and telegrams from angry women... and more than half of them were Republicans. Willkie lost.

When Roosevelt was re-elected, Frances offered her resignation. But FDR would not accept it. She was persistent, explaining on several occasions all the reasons she wanted to resign. Each time the president argued persuasively that they had formed an effective team, trusted one another, and told her she was needed. She did not want to leave him in the lurch. So, she relented.

The War

On a December Sunday in 1941, she was in New York for the weekend, hard at work on an important report when she got a phone call. It was the White House switchboard operator informing her that a cabinet meeting had been called for that night at 8:00. No details were given. She headed for the airport after gathering a few things. Other government officials were also there, boarding planes for Washington. No one knew what the urgency was. In 1941, the instant communication of news was still a long way off. Not until the cabinet was assembled, did they learn of the massive attack by hundreds of Japanese planes on Pearl Harbor, Hawaii, a

U.S. Navy base. Over 150 ships were destroyed and 2,500 civilians and servicemen killed. Though the declaration would be made by Congress officially the next day, everyone in the room knew that Americans would no longer be called "the Isolationists." The United States was at war.

The next day Frances went to her office before the President's address to Congress. She felt that her professional family, her Labor Department staff, could use a little encouragement and support at this frightening time on the brink of war. She told them, "We will find the strength to meet this."

As soon as the U.S. entered the war, unemployment completely disappeared. Men had joined the Armed Forces in droves. The opposite problem now emerged: there were more jobs than workers. And yet workers continued to go on strike. This caused resentment on the part of men fighting to preserve Democracy. Meanwhile, the two largest unions, the AFL and the CIO, were fiercely competing with one another, and constantly on a campaign for more members.

Frances had an idea. She urged FDR to call a conference, drawing together the major labor leaders and the employers most important to the war effort. After five days of discussions, all the leaders agreed to pledge themselves to a no-strike policy for the rest of the war. Meanwhile, they would, they agreed, settle disagreements by negotiation, with the understanding that a board appointed by President Roosevelt would make a decision in unsettled disputes, and all would agree to it.

It was critically important that they now had a united purpose. America required thousands of factories for all the airplanes, trucks, and tanks needed. These were built by the auto industry, while manufacturers of radios now turned out radar equipment. When Franklin told Frances that 50,000 new planes would be needed per year, she felt a bit faint, knowing that the previous year less than 1,000 had been built. As usual, the President was confident, and he turned out to be right. Within just four years, a finished plane was completed at the rate of one every five minutes! But overall, it took America's production rate less than one year to catch up to that of the enemy, the Axis powers, led by Germany.

How was it possible? After all, the majority of able-bodied men were overseas fighting. It's simple. For the first time in history, the country tapped a previously un-utilized resource: *women*. More than seven million of them went to work in

About to broadcast, soon after becoming Secretary of Labor.
In 1933 alone she made over 100 broadcasts
Public Domain

Time Magazine Cover, 1933,
with a charcoal portrait of Perkins

Time entitled the image
"Secretary of Labor" with her name
in tiny letters beneath.
The esteemed news magazine,
after 72 years of naming the
year's most influential person
"Man of the Year,"
took until 1999 to change
the honor to "Person of the Year."
In 2000 it released
"The 100 Women of the Year Project,
to recognize "influential women
who were often overshadowed"
and made Frances Perkins the
Woman of the Year for 1933.
This time the caption beneath her
photo read "Architect of the New Deal"
Public Domain

Frances arriving at the White House
Frances Perkins Center

With Carnegie Steel workers, 1933
Courtesy National Archives

Entering a mine shaft to inspect conditions, 1940
Frances Perkins papers, Columbia University

"The Anvil Chorus"- FDR and Frances
reacting to labor leaders fighting.
The title comes from the famous Verdi opera,
"Il Travatore" in which actual metal
anvils are struck with metal hammer heads
in the orchestra.
Political cartoon by Norman Ritchie, 1940.
Library of Congress

Ready to testify before Congress
on the Social Security Act
Library of Congress

Berryman Cartoon – Frances keeping a lid
on labor strikes when they threatened to boil
over under her administration
Public Domain

The Social Security Act Signing, August 14, 1935. Despite FDR's jubilation
and the legislation being her greatest achievement, Frances struggles to smile,
distraught over her husband's sudden disappearance from a mental hospital.
Courtesy FDR Presidential Library

Enjoying a visit with workers at the
Golden Gate Bridge construction site
in San Francisco, California, 1935
Courtesy Columbia University

A WPA Federal Art Project mural illustrating Labor
National Archives, FDR Library

Rosie the Riveter poster, 1942
Public Domain

A woman painting an insignia on a plane wing as part of the war effort, 1942
Heritage Images.

Welcoming FDR back from the December, 1943 Teheran conference of "The Big Three": FDR, Winston Churchill and Joseph Stalin. Their warm friendship and mutual sense of humor are apparent.
FDR Presidential Library and Museum

A small portion of the over seven acre FDR Memorial in Washington, D.C. unveiled in 1997. One of the FDR quotes reads "The test of our progress is not whether we add more to the abundance of those who have much. It is whether we provide enough for those who have too little."

Woman's Work Is Never Done

"Heigh Ho," one of two names given to this 1946 Herblock editorial cartoon, shows Frances starting work as the Civil Service Commissioner, at the insistence of President Truman. "Heigh Ho"("It's off to work we go!"), a tune from Walt Disney's 1937 film Snow White and the Seven Dwarfs, is sung as the seven head out for the mines. "Woman's Work" comes from a familiar saying: "A man's work is from sun to sun; but a woman's work is never done." Both reflect Frances's fierce work ethic. Even in her determined body language, marching to open yet another door, artist Herb Block depicted her commitment. That she is carrying her lunch box reflects it too. Far more often than not she ate meals at her desk and worked late to accomplish everything she could for her country's good

In front of Telluride House at
Cornell, 1963: Miss Perkins
is with Henry A. Wallace, who
had served with her on FDR's
cabinet as Secretary of
Agriculture, and been Vice
President from 1941 to 45.
With them is Telluride
student Bob King.
Courtesy of Christopher N. Breiseth

Lecturing at the Cornell School of International Labor Relations, late 1950's
Kheel Center, Cornell University

With Eleanor Roosevelt,
sharing a laugh following
the 1961 commemoration
of the 50th anniversary of the
Triangle Shirtwaist Factory fire
Kheel Center, Cornell University

Entertaining President
John F. Kennedy
following her speech at
the fiftieth anniversary
celebration of the
Department of Labor, 1963
The Frances Perkins Center

Tomlin Perkins Coggeshall
at his grandparents' grave,
Glidden Cemetery,
Newcastle, Maine
The Frances Perkins Center

The Frances Perkins
Center, and National
Historic Landmark
Homestead, today

war factories over the course of the next four years building whatever was needed. They produced everything from bullets to jeeps and bombers.

There is considerable disagreement over who first collectively called these workers by the name, "Rosie the Riveter." (Rivets were used to fasten metal plates together with a riveting gun.) And there is little agreement over who, if anyone, was the "real" inspiration for the 1942 poster of a working woman with her sleeve rolled up, under the banner "We Can Do It!" or who inspired the song "Rosie the Riveter" that came out in 1943. It was a peppy number, with lyrics that included,

All the day long whether rain or shine
She's a part of the assembly line
She's making history,
working for victory,
Rosie... the Riveter!

Also in 1943, famous illustrator Norman Rockwell painted a cover for *The Saturday Evening Post*, possibly after hearing the song. The worker he painted sports a riveting gun and a lunchbox labeled ROSIE.

But according to some biographers, it was actually Frances Perkins who first dubbed the iconic World War II heroic working woman "Rosie the Riveter."

Hordes of women also volunteered as nurses, in necessary service trades, and through organizations such as The American Red Cross. Very few stayed at home, as they'd been urged to do for centuries.

The President decided to shake up the usual order of the departments to meet the vast demands of the war. To do so he set up many separate, independent agencies. He felt that they should compete with one another for excellence, in turn inspiring workers in the war effort. He told Frances, "A little rivalry is stimulating, you know." It should not come as a surprise that to coordinate everything, he turned to his right-hand woman. "You take the lead in getting them together and keeping them together," he told her. Of course, she accepted the challenge, becoming a member of every committee, coordinating all the departments and agencies in Washington. At times she had to smooth over conflicts between them when the competition got too hot. This became her principal wartime occupation.

The Department of Labor, too, kept busy inspecting, investigating, and analyzing. She made sure each agency got the support and data they needed. In the course of the effort, Perkins perfected her skills as a mediator. It had always been her goal to get people to work together to achieve common goals for the good of the country. Now she knew she had succeeded. As usual, she gave the credit to the president, saying he inspired her to this achievement.

When FDR announced his run for a third term, it was unprecedented. But in 1944, with the U.S. still at war, he felt it important to run for yet a fourth term. The Allied forces which included the U.S. seemed to be winning, but no one wanted to risk a new leader in the midst of the struggle. They probably thought of the old saying, "Never change horses in the middle of the stream." Franklin had more than the war's end in mind. He wanted to be a part of a new world organization, one that would work to make peace a permanent reality. His dream was eventually realized in the creation of The United Nations.

Frances backed his decision to run again, but again resolved to resign. She even told her staff that by the start of the next term, the Labor Department would have a new head. She urged Roosevelt to announce her resignation at cabinet meetings, but he always put her off, saying they would talk about it another time. Everyone had seen the President age greatly in office, especially due to the unceasing strain of the war, during which he had little rest, exercise, or sleep. Only just before his fourth inauguration did Frances become frightened by his appearance. His hands were shaking, his color was poor, and he looked completely exhausted.

The President had called a cabinet meeting for the day before Inauguration Day. Frances offered to type out the resignation letter herself and hand it to the press secretary. She had thought he would accept it this time. She fully expected he would announce her departure at the meeting. When he did not, she asked to see him afterwards. When they were finally seated face to face, she sensed "his enormous fatigue." She hated to press him, but felt she had to.

"Don't you think I had better get the press secretary to announce my resignation right now?" she began.

"No," he said. "Frances, you can't go now. You mustn't put this on me now. I can't think of anybody else, and I can't get used to anybody else. Not now! Do stay there and don't say anything."

Although it was an effort for him to speak, he next spoke words she would never forget. In the way he said them, she realized he was speaking his feelings from the heart.

"Frances, you have done awfully well. I know what you have been through. I know what you have accomplished. Thank you." He grasped her hand. She had a strong sense that this was their last real conversation.

She wrote in her biography of him, "He put his hand over mine and gripped it. There were tears in our eyes.... It was all the reward that I could ever have asked." She knew he was grateful. Years afterward, upon leaving office, she told a colleague that following this last, heartfelt private chat with her old friend Franklin, she felt that "my cup runneth over." It was a quote from the 23rd Psalm, a favorite of hers.

A short time later he flew to Yalta, in the Ukraine, for a final conference of "the Big Three" Allied leaders, with Winston Churchill of Great Britain and Joseph Stalin of Russia. Frances was alarmed when Franklin later told her he was planning yet another trip, in the spring, to England with Eleanor, "to see the British people myself." She protested that traveling there during the war was far too dangerous. He confided in her one final time, in a whisper: "The war in Europe will be over by the end of May."

But the month before the planned trip to England, President Roosevelt died. Frances took great comfort in the fact that at the very end of his life, he had been certain that the long war he had worked so hard to shepherd America through was about to end.

The year following his death, Frances Perkins published her second book, *The Roosevelt I Knew*. It was a best-seller and is still considered by many the most intimate and thorough biography of Franklin Delano Roosevelt ever written.

Chapter 15

A New Leaf

Frances had served her country as the Secretary of Labor for twelve years, far longer than anyone else in that position before or since. Yet the new President, Harry Truman, asked her to stay on for a while to smooth the transition. After she had done that, he still would not let her resign completely from the government. She requested that she be made head of the Social Security Administration, a supremely logical appointment. But Truman was insistent that she accept the post of Civil Service Commissioner, as an important male supporter had requested Social Security. Frances acceded to the president's wishes.

So, she remained in Washington, still a public servant. She held that position for seven more years, submitting her final resignation on the day President Eisenhower was inaugurated, January 20th, 1953.

It was a difficult time of transition for Frances. At the end of 1952, her husband Paul Wilson had suffered a stroke and died. Her relationship with her daughter, who had divorced after an unhappy and chaotic marriage, was a difficult one. Sadly, Susanna had inherited the bipolar disorder her father had suffered from. She had a number of emotional breakdowns, the first occurring when she was a college student, forcing her to withdraw from school. Never fully facing up to her illness, she tended to blame her mother for all the problems life posed. At one point, she faulted her mother not for giving her too little love, but too much. She complained that if she had not been an only child, Frances would have had to divide her motherly attentions, which Susanna did not always appreciate.

Things improved after Susanna married again, this time to a gifted artist who had three children of his own. They moved to Connecticut, and in 1954, presented Frances with her one and only grandchild, Tomlin Perkins Coggeshall. The new grandma was ecstatic. She lavished attention and affection on the handsome little blue-eyed boy whenever possible and called him "a model of quiet nerves and amiable disposition."

When her work in Washington was over, she was 73 years old. One would have thought she would retire to her beloved homestead on the coast of Maine to write her memoirs and spend time with her grandchild. But Frances Perkins was not the retiring kind! She was too accustomed to having challenges before her and always strongly felt that there was "still so much work to be done." And she still needed an income to support herself.

So it was that in her seventies, she embarked on a whole new career. Invited to lecture at a number of colleges, she first chose the University of Illinois, where she was well paid to both lecture and conduct twelve seminars on the history of the labor movement. Preparing carefully, she turned the opportunity into a big success. The word spread, and other colleges and universities competed to have her visit.

After two years on the lecture circuit, however, she began to feel lonely. She had lived and worked in Washington for 22 years, but felt the need to finally move back east and be closer to her family and old friends, including some Mount Holyoke classmates. The move was not without misgivings. She had given her own Manhattan apartment to Susanna for her family of six, and had to rent a room in a close friend's apartment.

But the move did not lift her spirits. Her declining health contributed to her problems, as she coped with high blood pressure and other ailments associated with aging. She wondered if she could summon the strength necessary to accept an invitation to lecture in two European cities. But she went anyway, and her reception there and the huge success of her lectures buoyed her. She also accepted lecture engagements commemorating the 25th anniversary of the Social Security Act, and the 50th anniversary commemoration of the Triangle Shirtwaist Factory fire which had been such a catalyst in her life.

Just Desserts

The real turning point occurred when Frances visited Cornell University in upstate New York to lecture on the future of the labor movement in the U.S. Cornell was a perfect fit. The university already had a School of Industrial and Labor Relations. Her 1955 visit was such a hit that within just a few months Cornell invited her to join the faculty on a permanent basis, with specific responsibilities, while still allowing her the freedom to lecture elsewhere.

It was a lucky day for Cornell when they made the decision to employ her. She brought not only a treasure trove of experience to the job, but a wealth of colorful first-hand history. With her amazingly detailed memory, she could entrance students and faculty with her accounts of Jane Addams and Hull House, the Triangle Shirtwaist fire, the women's suffrage movement, the Great Depression and World Wars I and II, not to mention all the ins and outs of the many administrative terms she'd served in. In one lecture on her former boss, Governor Al Smith, she drew on her early acting talents, bringing him colorfully alive using his accent and gestures and describing his attire. She made his transformation from a boy working in the Fulton Fish Market of New York into a national leader an inspiring example of what one can achieve. Her audience stood and cheered.

At Cornell, for the first time in her life, Frances was able to save, invest, and build some wealth. Yet she never indulged herself. As with many people who had lived through the Great Depression, she fretted over spending money, denying herself any luxuries. She was determined to leave behind enough resources when she died that her grandson's education would be fully provided for.

Five years after first appearing on the Cornell campus, she received an astonishing invitation. The university had a group called the Telluride Association which provided special housing for top male students, whether undergraduates or graduate students. All were there on fellowships they'd been awarded for their exceptional scholastic achievements. It was not a stretch to call these young men Cornell's intellectual elite. No woman had ever lived at Telluride House, their special residence. But their young president, Christopher Breiseth, had the idea that the first should be the number one career woman in the nation's history. The others agreed that they wanted Frances to have that honor. At a dinner at Telluride, the young men "popped the question." She was thrilled. Frances told a professor friend and his wife, "Do you know what those boys at Telluride have done? They have asked me to come and live with them. I feel like a bride!"

It was a fitting honor and reward, and one that brought her joy. At many turns in the long road to changing America for the better, she had been labeled a radical, a socialist, or a communist. She had been often ridiculed behind her back or in the press. Even after leaving the federal government, she was considered a controversial figure by many. But in her golden years, she gradually came to be widely viewed with respect. Many in Washington and across the country considered her a wise elder stateswoman.

If Frances's life had been a banquet, Cornell University and Telluride House were the dessert. From 1960 on, being surrounded by the young gave her nothing less than the gift of a new lease on life. Telluride offered companionship with stimulating conversation, and a lovely, spacious home in which she could entertain.

She had no official duties, housekeeping or otherwise, but became a beloved presence and favorite confidante. Before they knew it, the students saw her bring their neglected flower garden beautifully back to life. She had a passion for heirloom flowers, some of which bloomed at The Brick House. She taught the boys how to throw a sherry party and the proper way to eat a Maine lobster at dinners she hosted. She began to dress, once again, with feminine flair. Her relaxed but elegant manners rubbed off on the young men. Affection flowed in both directions. The other residents, all in their late teens and twenties, not only benefitted from Frances's presence, but loved her dry sense of humor and her piercing insights. One later admitted, "She was so unassuming and unpretentious that it was easy to underestimate her. It took us a while to realize just how sharp she was."

In the noisy environment of the house, with up to thirty young men bounding up and down the stairs day and night, it was probably a blessing that she was losing her hearing. But Frances forged lasting ties, becoming closer to many of the students than their own parents and grandparents were. She was a great listener, friend, and mentor.

Frances became something of the campus rock star. When she hosted a reception for President Truman at Cornell, he entered the room and promptly kissed her, declaring that beside his wife, mother, and daughter, Miss Perkins was the only person in the world he kissed. Her Mount Holyoke classmates also seemed to bask in her star power. She found their reunions a joy, and felt indebted to them in return. One classmate called her their "polished cornerstone" and another wrote, "You are the focal point that has held us all together."

Meanwhile, with the support of Cornell, she began work on a second major biography to be entitled, *The Al Smith I Knew*. She was never to finish it. Among other challenges, her eyesight had been declining for many years.

She still thoroughly enjoyed a good long stay at the Newcastle, Maine family homestead every summer, a life-long tradition. There she particularly relished visits from her daughter and delighted in her grandson as he grew. She was a superb grandmother, often taking young Tomlin on outings. He has particularly fond memories of an occasion when he was about eight. She took him to see the model trains running, and pick out a toy, at F.A.O. Schwartz, the famous Manhattan toy store. After treating him to lunch, she took him to the train station, where he was impressed by her lengthy and knowledgeable conversations with the conductor and engineer. Clearly, they felt they were being visited by royalty.

In the winter that spanned 1964 and 1965, she was nearly 85 years old, and realized her health was in decline. She was frail, nearly deaf, and completely blind in one eye, with limited vision in the other.

Not wanting to face a forced retirement, she began considering other living arrangements. She did not feel that moving in with either Susanna or her sister Ethel was an option. Nor could she manage the harsh, snowy winters and isolation of the Brick House alone. Following a spring trip to Washington, D.C. to visit old friends and have one final retreat at All Saints Convent, she returned to New York City, where she stayed in her friend's rented room.

A short time later she was admitted to the hospital with an enlarged heart. The diagnosis was sadly apt for a woman whose big heart had always taken in those most in need, and who had devoted her life to public service. A series of strokes and a coma quickly followed. Her death came on May 14th, 1965.

One service was not enough. First all her Cornell friends organized an Episcopal memorial service there. Her old friend Professor Neufeld delivered a tribute, recalling her vibrant personality, courage, gift for friendship, and her religious spirit, out of which grew her "sense of duty and inner discipline, which increased with the years and formed the central core of her character." He said she'd lived by her grandmother's motto: "When in doubt, do what is right."

Her funeral was held in New York City, with many friends and colleagues coming from afar, including Albany and Washington. It was a formal Requiem Mass at her small New York church and was attended by the State Industrial Commissioner as well as the U.S. Secretary of Labor. The pallbearers who carried her were eight close friends, all young men from Telluride House. Their grief was written on their faces. The minister used the same text from the book of First Corinthians that Frances had used for her last speech at Mount Holyoke, in 1902, which included the class motto, "Be ye Stedfast." The commandment, written by St. Paul, one of Jesus's disciples over 2,000 years ago, was more than a slogan. It was her life's story.

The service was perfect. After all, she had arranged it herself two decades earlier and left detailed instructions for the minster officiating. She had chosen three Bible readings, all from the Book of Psalms, feeling that they would reflect the meaning of her life's work.

She was buried just a short walk from her beloved saltwater farm along the Damariscotta River in Newcastle, Maine, at the family cemetery. Her headstone is between her husband's and those of her parents. It is a simple stone, with a cross at the top, carved simply, as she instructed,

FRANCES PERKINS WILSON
1880-1965
SECRETARY OF LABOR OF U.S.A.
1933-1945

Chapter 16
The World after Frances

During her lifetime, Frances had bestowed on her many honorary degrees and other awards and citations. Some of these, given her modesty, had been stowed away in a barn attic above a corn crib in Newcastle, and not rediscovered until preservation work began on the Brick House and Homestead in 2022. One, now framed and on display, was an award for distinguished service from the United States Department of Labor upon its 50th anniversary, and spoke of her courage, strength, and "her spirit in waging the good fight."

Another was a citation from the International Association of Labor Officials, which ended with wording that summed up her character beautifully: "For her never-failing belief that progress can come through the united efforts of men and women of good will, for her appreciation of the importance of the individual, and for the kindliness of spirit and the human touch which she brought to all her endeavors."

Unsurprisingly, Frances's death was followed by many more testimonials, tributes, and honors. The then current Labor Secretary praised her achievements, and Mount Holyoke began a scholarship and a graduate fellowship in her name. The first of several biographies appeared a year later. Greater honors took time. In 1980, Congress named the newly built United States Department of Labor headquarters The Frances Perkins Building, prominently displayed on its facade. In the same year, the U.S. Post Office honored her with a stamp. In 1982 she was inducted into the National Women's Hall of Fame, and in 1988 into the Labor Hall of Fame.

Then in 1995 the Episcopal Church held a conference to mark the 60th anniversary of Social Security. Donn Mitchell, a professor of ethics and religion, had this to say about Frances in a resolution at the conference:

Perhaps no other American had greater impact on the provision of human and social services, the relief of misery, and the creation of safe and just working conditions. As both a woman who set precedents and as a layperson who effectively answered a call from God, she represents the best of the 20th century Church.

In 2008, Frances was named a "notable saint" by the Episcopal Church. The following year May 13th was set as her feast day, commemorating her as a Public Servant, for having "sought to build a society in which all may live in health and decency."

Also in 2008 the Frances Perkins Center was founded by her grandson, Tomlin Perkins Coggeshall and others, headquartered in Damariscotta, Maine, about two miles from The Brick House. Its purpose is to preserve Frances's legacy and ensure that she and her work are not only remembered, but become more widely known. Annually the center chooses outstanding individuals to recognize for their achievements and contributions in carrying on the mission of Frances Perkins, and celebrates those recognized ceremoniously at the homestead.

The remaining 57-acre property of The Frances Perkins Homestead was listed as a National Historic Landmark in 2014. In that year, St. Andrew's Episcopal Church in Newcastle was gifted with a beautiful hand-painted icon, a plaque picturing Frances as an Episcopal saint, in her iconic tricorn hat. In the sanctuary is another plaque commemorating her important presence in the St. Andrew's congregation. Frances had worshipped at the beautiful little half-timbered church overlooking the Damariscotta River for 60 years, whenever she was in Maine.

In 2020 Tomlin Coggeshall, who had inherited the property from his mother Susanna, sold it to the Frances Perkins Center. For the next two years, necessary renovations were made to The Brick House and its extensive attached barns, following years of fundraising. In the next phase, more millions will be raised to build an adjacent Educational Center on the property. The invitation to the 2023 Opening Celebration of the Frances Perkins Homestead National Historic Landmark, read,

The Frances Perkins Center honors the legacy of Frances Perkins by sharing her commitment to the principle that government should provide all its people with the best possible life, and by preserving the place that shaped her character.

The Center convenes leaders and future leaders in public policy, labor and related fields to generate creative solutions to today's social and economic problems and teaches students of all ages about a remarkable woman whose work continues to improve the lives of ordinary Americans.

Summing up the life of a person who gave us so much is not easy. Nor was Frances's life easy. One earlier biographer referred to the "fragile balancing act of her personal life." Supporting a husband with a mental illness requiring regular hospitalization was a strain both emotionally and financially. At the highest moment of her career, the very day of the Social Security Act signing, she had received an emergency phone call. Instead of celebrating her huge achievement with her colleagues, she hailed a cab to catch a train to New York. Her husband had gone missing, having wandered away from a sanitarium. She dropped everything to go search for him the moment the signing was completed. With the help of friends, Paul Wilson was thankfully found safe. This kind of crisis always seemed to lurk just around the corner in her life. And yet she carried on.

The light of inspiration was a torch she passed to many her life had touched. One of her young pallbearers was to become president of the World Bank, and served the defense department as Deputy Secretary. Another, Dr. Christopher N. Breiseth, became a foremost scholar of the New Deal and the director of the Franklin and Eleanor Roosevelt Institute in Hyde Park, New York, where they had lived.

Of course, she also greatly inspired countless others paving the way for girls and women of future generations. All Americans owe her a debt of gratitude. It brings to mind a Chinese proverb: "When you are drinking the water, never forget who dug the well."

Her legacy lies not just in the New Deal achievements she brought about, but in the regularly updated codes that protect workers in offices and factories everywhere. Today few people appreciate how different life was before Frances Perkins. We take for granted that children can go to school, not mills or coal mines every day; that people work for eight hours, not fifteen; that they get paid "time and a half" for overtime; that they can receive checks when unemployed or disabled; that they needn't dread the day when they can no longer work. Over seventy million Americans receive benefits under Social Security every month. The figure includes retirees, survivors, dependents, and the disabled.

There was only one priority item on her famous wish list she presented to FDR before becoming Secretary of Labor that she and the New Deal were not able to fulfill. It was universal health care. She left us a single major unfilled goal, one we as a nation are still striving to realize.

In his introduction to a new edition of *The Roosevelt I Knew*, Adam Cohen, an author and Yale law professor, wrote that Perkins was "a brilliant self-creation," and that she was as important an icon as Benjamin Franklin or Thomas Paine, and that like them, she had helped to start a revolution. Before the unique partnership of Roosevelt and Perkins came to Washington, he noted, the federal government had done little more than defend the country and deliver the mail. And of course, tax its citizens.

In the final chapter of his recent book *Tread the City's Streets Again: Frances Perkins Shares her Theology*, Donn Mitchell wrote that she was "indeed steadfast in her life in the church... (and) was also steadfast in her work, overcoming the barriers of a woman in a man's world and establishing safeguards for human life and dignity that remain in place on a national scale to this day."

That her name has so little recognition today is due in part to her well-guarded privacy and her extreme modest humility throughout life. What she did was not for personal credit or fame, but done selflessly. She labored out of a deep thirst for social justice and a desire to live out her faith's great commandment to love one another. She worked for the good of all, present and future. If the history books later gave almost all of the credit to Franklin D. Roosevelt, perhaps it would not have disturbed her.

It would be two decades before another woman was appointed to a Presidential cabinet. Not until the 1990s were there more than two or three women in the U.S. Senate at any given time. Discrimination against women, like racism, dies slowly. Women in our society still have a long way to go before true equality is reached.

When rock-star Supreme Court Justice Ruth Bader Ginsberg, AKA "Notorious RBG," graduated from law school at the top of her class in 1959, having achieved the honor of making the prestigious *Law Review* at both Harvard and Columbia, no law firm would hire her because of her gender.

The Equal Rights Amendment was first proposed to Congress by Alice Paul in 1923. Despite years of dedicated activism, it has never been added to our Constitution.

Though almost 60 countries worldwide have had a female head of state, the United States is still not among them.

When Barack Obama became President, his first executive order of January 2009 was signing the Lily Ledbetter Fair Pay Act, to right the wrong of unreasonable time limits placed on Lily's — and other women's — right to sue for equal pay for equal work. Women continue to experience a gender pay gap, which is narrowing very slowly, earning on average about 80 cents for every dollar men make for comparable work.

We stand on the shoulders of our foremothers. It is a gift to be able to look for inspiration to those who came before us, making inroads and opening doors. There are many such pioneering women, though it is hard to find one who did nearly as much as Frances Perkins for her country's good.

Now that you know the woman behind all these achievements, you can help to spread the word about an American Superstar whose name few people know. She has shown us how much can be accomplished in one lifetime. Who knows what wonderful things you may yet contribute with yours?

Seeds, Sparks and Sources of Inspiration

Frances's Top Ten

1. Her faith and its commandment to love one another.

2. Florence Kelley, who spoke at Mount Holyoke in 1902.

3. Factory field trips in Holyoke, Massachusetts.

4. Jacob Riis's book *How the Other Half Lives*.

5. Hull House and other settlement houses.

6. Theodore Roosevelt and his commitment to social progress.

7. Philadelphia, where she began to recognize and use her gifts.

8. The bakeries and factories of Hell's Kitchen, New York.

9. The Triangle Shirtwaist Factory fire and Rose Schneiderman's speech.

10. The Great Depression and its aftermath and defeat.

Each of these experiences and influences helped prepare her for all she achieved in Chicago, Philadelphia, New York City, Albany, and then Washington, DC.

The Wit and Wisdom Of Frances Perkins

It is kind of grubby going around with politicians unless you happen to enjoy the human race in its many peculiar aspects.

Feminism means revolution, and I am a revolutionist.

On her father's lack of compliments:

Even if I had ever succeeded in making myself look pretty — which, mind you, I'm not saying I ever succeeded in doing — my father would have never told me. That would have been a sin.

Of Teddy Roosevelt, to his daughter, Alice Roosevelt Longworth:

He had been the first to reach the peak of political life who pointed out a social obligation: the sufferings of the poor, of the oppressed, of the immigrants, and the right and duty of those with advantages to do something about it.

Of hecklers at speeches:

I learned the advantage of a little funny story — very short, very pointed, very harmless, not derogatory to anybody. It's a trick that's stood by me many times.

Of the Triangle fire:

The scene struck at the pit of my stomach. I felt I must sear it not only on my mind but on my heart as a never-to-be-forgotten reminder of why I had to spend my life fighting conditions that could permit such a tragedy.

Upon accepting the unsalaried position of executive secretary of the Maternity Center Association:

What social projects I did I took up because at the moment they moved me very deeply. Nobody else was there to do it, and I did it.

On activism:

I think that 50 people with a determination to do something right can start forces that have their strength largely because of the moral appeal of what it is they're recommending.

On observing FDR's courage:

I began to see what the great teachers of religion meant when they said that humility is the greatest of virtues, and that if you can't learn it, God will teach it to you by humiliation.

To a reporter who asked if being labor commissioner wouldn't be harder for a woman than a man:

Being a woman has only bothered me in climbing trees.

Explaining why she accepted the job as FDR's Secretary of Labor, at great personal cost:

The door might not be opened to a woman again for a long, long time, and I had a kind of duty to other women to walk in and sit down on the chair that was offered, and so establish the right of others long hence and far distant in geography to sit in the high seats.

After accepting the post of Labor Secretary, to FDR:

Now Governor, if between now and Inauguration Day you change your mind about this, or if you find there is objection on the part of the politicians, or ...for any reason at all... don't give me a moment's thought. Just tell me it is all over, and that's fine.

On FDR's empathy, shown in his Fireside Chats:

When he talked on the radio, he saw them gathered in their little parlor, listening with their neighbors. His face would smile and light up as though he were actually… with them. In particular, he wanted to talk about what could be done to make this a better, more beautiful, and more sustaining country.

On the coming of the Great Depression:

But with the slow menace of a glacier, Depression came on. No one had any measure of its progress; no one had any plan for stopping it. Everyone tried to get out of its way.

On tackling the Great Depression:

It is there to be done, so I do it.

On her approach to work:

Doing means digging your nails in and working like a truck horse. We make most of our own opportunities. They seldom make us.

On unwinding:

A weekly swim in the summer and a walk in the woods in winter keeps me straight.

On spending time at the convent in Maryland:

I have discovered the rule of silence is one of the most beautiful things in the world. It gives one time for so many, many ideas and occupations. It also preserves one from the temptation of the idle word, the fresh remark, the wisecrack, the angry challenge, the hot-tempered reaction, the argument about nothing, the foolish question, the unnecessary noise of the human click-clack.

At a celebration of the 25th anniversary of Social Security:

One thing I know: Social Security is so firmly embedded in the American psychology today that no politician, no political party... could possibly destroy this Act and still maintain our democratic system. It is safe forever, and for the everlasting benefit of the people of the United States.

And finally, perhaps her most famous quote:

I came to Washington to work for God, FDR, and the millions of forgotten, plain, common working men.

(Note: Until at least the 1970's "*men*" was commonly used to mean all people, male and female.)

Acknowledgments

I am indebted and grateful to the following people for the gift of their generous time and assistance, which has made this book possible:

Tomlin Coggeshall and Christopher Rice, whose many invitations and warm hospitality enabled me to become steeped in the history and atmosphere of The Brick House, grounds, and Frances's story.

My first readers, Jennifer Bunting, Valerie Haskins, Kate Philbin, Mari Wallace, Susan Easter, Sarah Peskin, and Mackenzie Philbin, for their invaluable feedback.

The board and staff of the Frances Perkins Center, especially Michael Chaney, Laura Chaney, Emma Wegner, Sarah Peskin, Susan Easter, and Giovanna Gray Lockhart, Susan Bateson, Peter Blaze Corcoran, Leah Sprague, and Christopher Breiseth

Histria Books, my publisher, and particularly Dana Ungureanu, Diana Livesay, Audrey Weinbrecht, and Dr. Kurt Brackob.

The supportive writers of my blurbs, Christopher N. Breiseth, Mick Caouette, Tomlin Coggeshall, Sarah Peskin, and Mackenzie Philbin.

And of course, John Longmaid, the FPC's first and foremost benefactor, whose constant enthusiasm, love, support and patience can never be measured.

Bibliography

Major Sources:

Coleman, Penny. *A Woman Unafraid: The Achievements of Frances Perkins*. New York: Atheneum, 1993.

Downey, Kirstin. *The Woman Behind the New Deal: The Life and Legacy of Frances Perkins*. New York: Anchor Books, 2009.

Frances Perkins Center. *A Promise to all Generations: Stories & Essays about Social Security & Frances Perkins*. Newcastle, ME: 2011.

Gore Schiff, Karenna. *Lighting the Way: Nine Women Who Changed Modern America,* Frances Perkins chapter, pp. 130-189, 2005.

Keller, Emily. *Frances Perkins, First Woman Cabinet Member*. Greensboro, NC: Morgan Reynolds Publishing, 2006.

Lawson, Don. *Frances Perkins, First Lady of the Cabinet*. New York, Abelard-Schuman, 1966.

Martin, George. *Madam Secretary*. Boston: Houghton Mifflin Co. 1976.

Mitchell, Donn. *Tread the City's Streets Again: Frances Perkins Shares Her Theology*. Princeton, NJ: Anglican Examiner Publications, 2018.

Pasachoff, Naomi. *Frances Perkins, Champion of the New Deal*. New York, Oxford University Press, 1999.

Perkins, Frances. *People At Work*: New York: The John Day Company, 1934, reprint Delhi, India: Facsimile Publisher, 2018.

— *The Roosevelt I Knew*, New York: Viking Press, 1946, New York: Penguin Group, introduction by Adam Cohen, 2011.

— *Reminiscences* — audio autobiography, Columbia University Oral History Research Office Collection, 1950's

Secondary and E-Sources

Caouette, Mick. *Summoned: Frances Perkins and the General Welfare*. South Hill Films. 2020

Cole, Arlene McCurda. *History Tales of Newcastle, Maine*. Lincoln County Publishing, 2012.

Chronicles of Lincoln County, compiled by R.B. Fillmore. Augusta, ME: Kennebec Journal Print Shop,1924.

Crew, Spencer R. "The Great Migration." *Encyclopedia Virginia.org*. Accessed 12/12/2018.

Neil, Patrick. "Life in Hooverville." June 11, 2016. *TheVintageNews.com*. Accessed 12/18/18

Walsh, Kenneth. February 12, 2009. "The First 100 Days: Franklin Roosevelt Pioneered the 100-Day Concept." *U.S.* "1900-1929 Progressive Era to New Era." *Library of Congress, LOC.gov*. Accessed 12/22/18.

"Great Depression History." *www.History.com*. Accessed 1/12/2019

"Highlights from the Life and Legacy of Frances Perkins." Film by the Frances Perkins Center, Newcastle, Maine, A Parons Bend Production. 2019.

Images of America: Along the Damariscotta River, compiled by Dorothy A. Blanchard. Maine: Arcadia Publishing, 1995. Accessed 1/ 5/ 2019.

"More than 140 die as flames..." March 26, 1911. *The New York Tribune*. Accessed 3/13/19.

Places to Visit

1. "The Brick House," the Frances Perkins Homestead, and the Frances Perkins Center, River Road, Newcastle, Maine. Tours available through the Frances Perkins Center.

2. Glidden Cemetery, River Road, Newcastle, Maine.

3. St. Andrew's Episcopal Church, Glidden Street, Newcastle, Maine.

4. The Frances Perkins Building, Department of Labor, 200 Constitution Avenue NW, Washington, D.C.

5. Frances Perkins House, 16 Cottage Street, Worcester, Massachusetts.

6. Springwood, Home of Franklin D. and Eleanor Roosevelt, Hyde Park, New York.